Ela Area Public Library District
275 Mohawk Trail, Lake Zurich, IL 60047
(847) 438-3433
www.eapl.org

31241008403316

JUL – – 2015

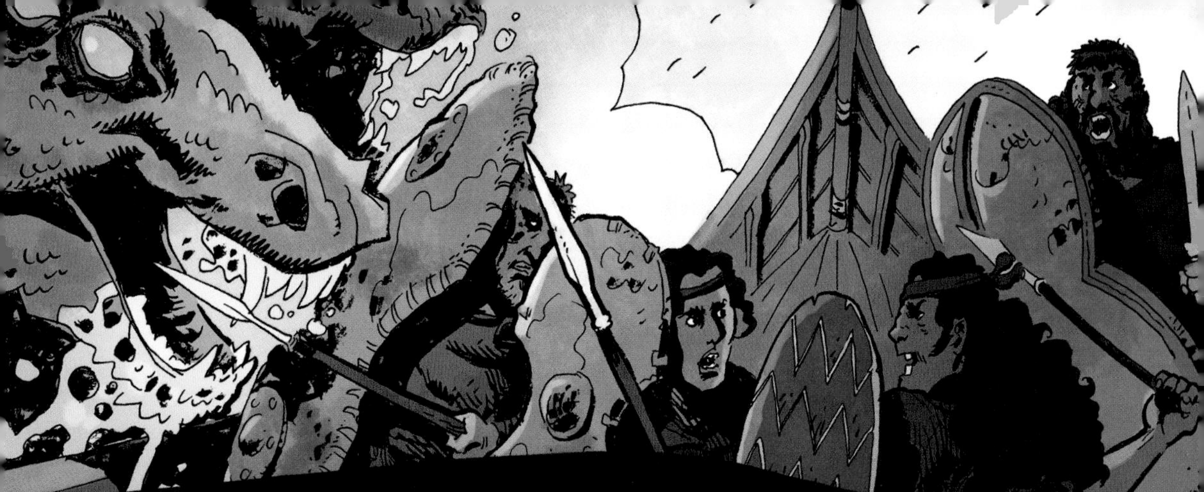

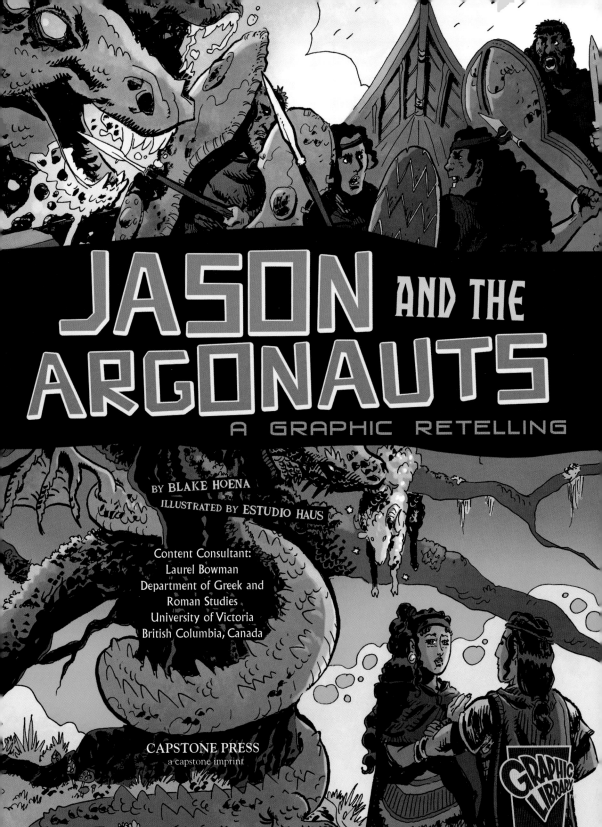

JASON AND THE ARGONAUTS

A GRAPHIC RETELLING

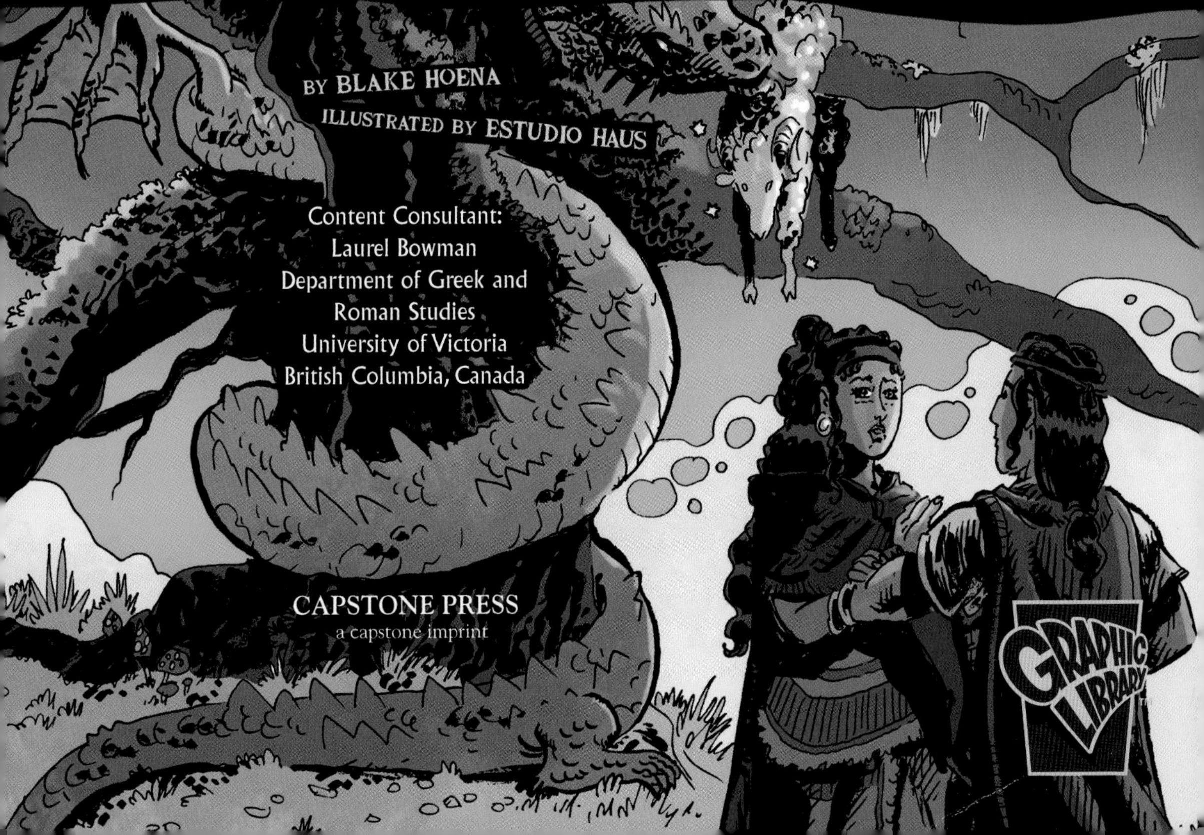

BY BLAKE HOENA

ILLUSTRATED BY ESTUDIO HAUS

Content Consultant:
Laurel Bowman
Department of Greek and
Roman Studies
University of Victoria
British Columbia, Canada

CAPSTONE PRESS
a capstone imprint

GRAPHIC LIBRARY

Graphic Library is published by Capstone Press,
1710 Roe Crest Drive, North Mankato, Minnesota 56003
www.capstonepub.com

Library of Congress Cataloging-in-Publication Data
Hoena, B. A., author.
  Jason and the Argonauts : a graphic retelling / by Blake Hoena ; illustrated by Estudio Haus.
      pages cm.—(Graphic library. Ancient myths)
  Summary: "The story of Jason and the Argonauts told in graphic novel format"—Provided by
publisher.
  Audience: Ages 8-14.
  Audience: Grades 4 to 6.
  Includes bibliographical references and index.
  ISBN 978-1-4914-2072-0 (library binding)
  ISBN 978-1-4914-2276-2 (paperback)
  ISBN 978-1-4914-2290-8 (eBook pdf)
1. Jason (Greek mythology)—Comic books, strips, etc. 2. Jason (Greek mythology)—Juvenile
literature. 3. Argonauts (Greek mythology)—Comic books, strips, etc. 4. Argonauts (Greek
mythology)—Juvenile literature. 5. Mythology, Greek—Comic books, strips, etc. 6. Mythology,
Greek—Juvenile literature. I. Estudio Haus (Firm) illustrator. II. Title.
  BL820.A8H64 2015
  398.2'0938—dc23   2014018940

Editor
Anthony Wacholtz

Art Director
Nathan Gassman

Designer
Ashlee Suker

Production Specialist
Tori Abraham

Printed in the United States of America in Stevens Point, Wisconsin
092014   008479WZS15

TABLE OF CONTENTS

ORIGINS OF THE MYTH

The story of Jason and the Argonauts was recorded in *Argonautica* by Rhodius Apollonius, a poet who lived during the third century B.C. His story tells of a large gathering of heroes who set off to find a priceless treasure, the golden fleece. This adaptation is based on Apollonius' version of the Argonauts' quest.

A HERO IN TRAINING

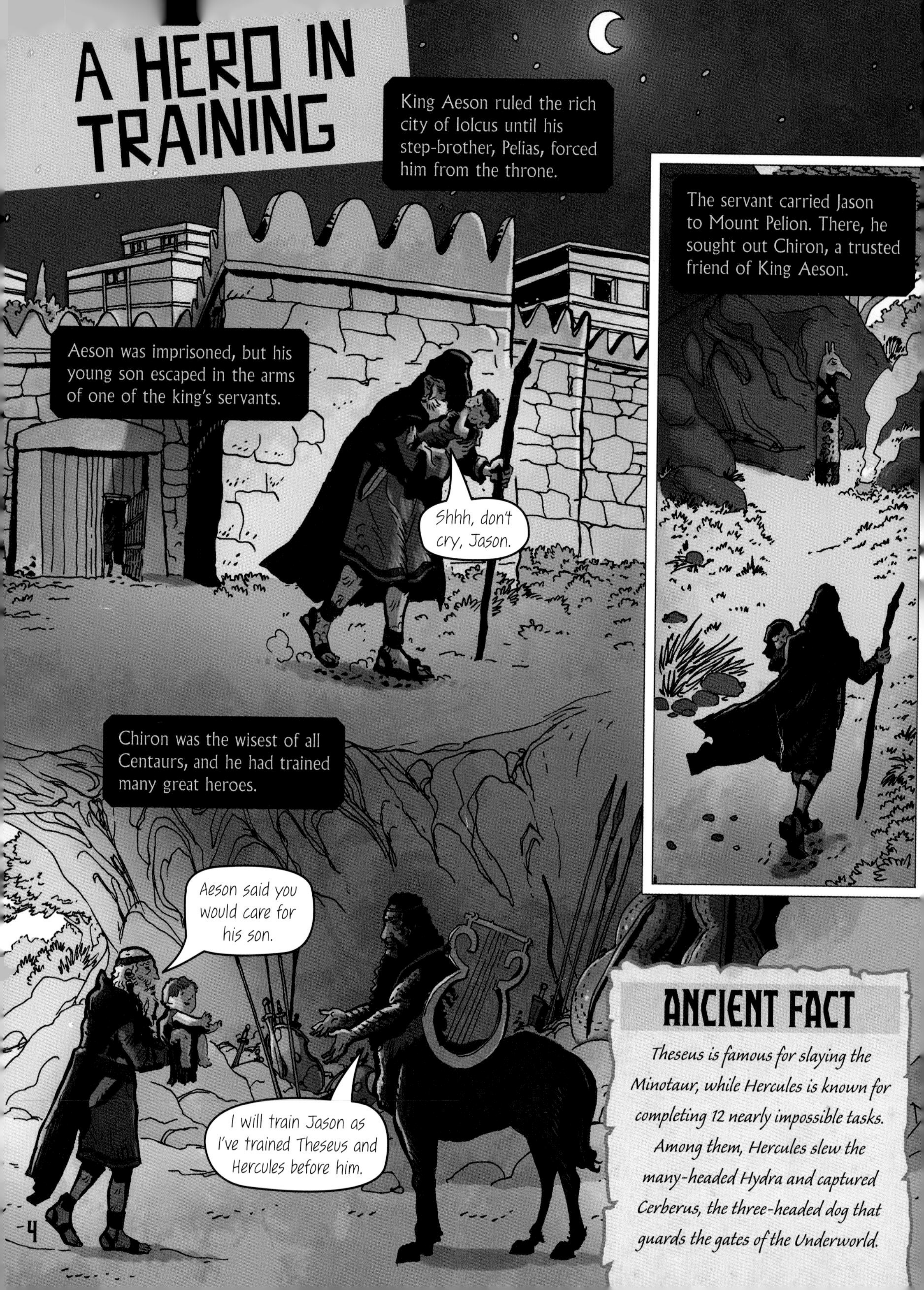
King Aeson ruled the rich city of Iolcus until his step-brother, Pelias, forced him from the throne.
Aeson was imprisoned, but his young son escaped in the arms of one of the king's servants.
Shhh, don't cry, Jason.
The servant carried Jason to Mount Pelion. There, he sought out Chiron, a trusted friend of King Aeson.
Chiron was the wisest of all Centaurs, and he had trained many great heroes.
Aeson said you would care for his son.
I will train Jason as I've trained Theseus and Hercules before him.

ANCIENT FACT

Theseus is famous for slaying the Minotaur, while Hercules is known for completing 12 nearly impossible tasks. Among them, Hercules slew the many-headed Hydra and captured Cerberus, the three-headed dog that guards the gates of the Underworld.

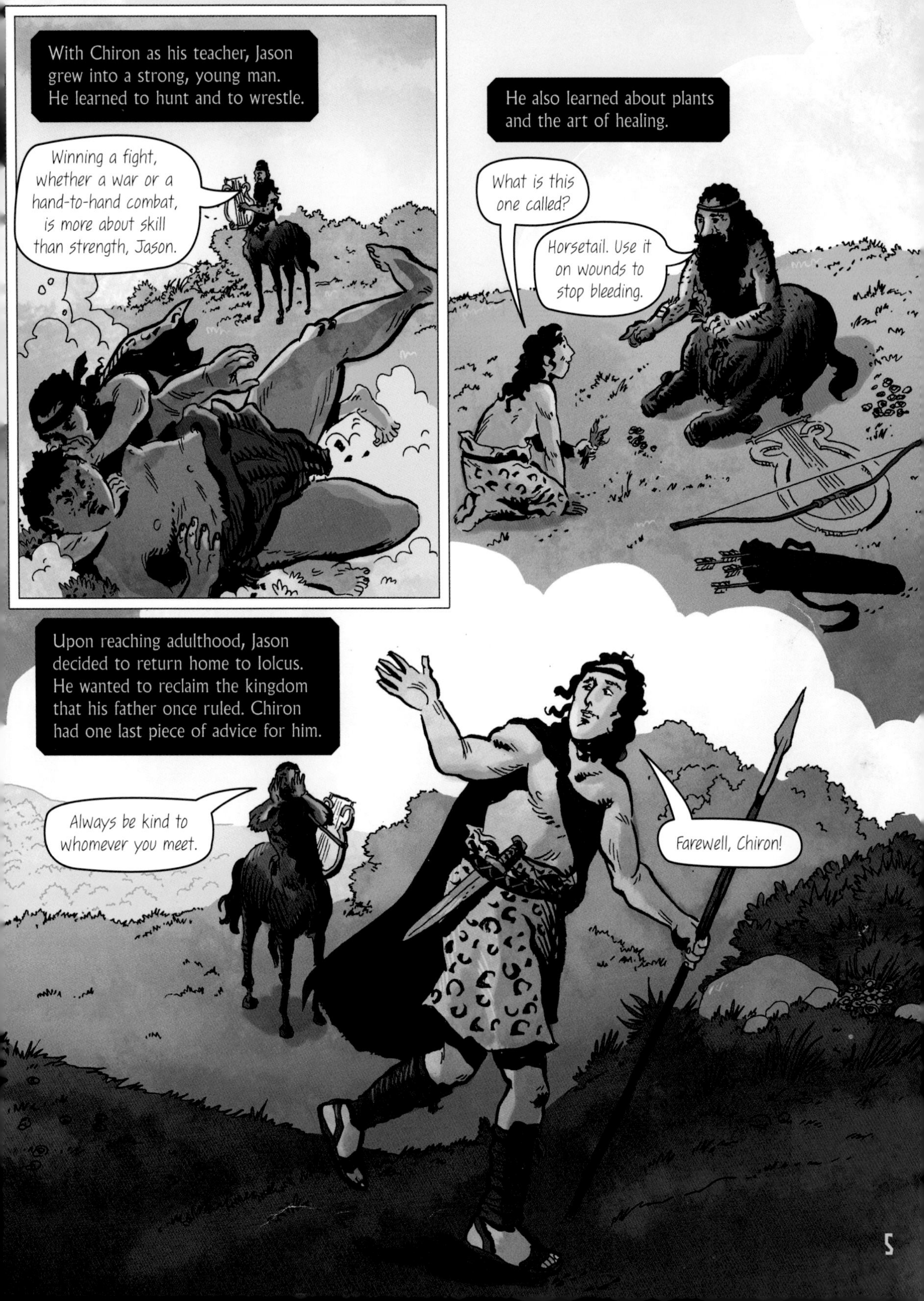

With Chiron as his teacher, Jason grew into a strong, young man. He learned to hunt and to wrestle.
Winning a fight, whether a war or a hand-to-hand combat, is more about skill than strength, Jason.
He also learned about plants and the art of healing.
What is this one called?
Horsetail. Use it on wounds to stop bleeding.
Upon reaching adulthood, Jason decided to return home to Iolcus. He wanted to reclaim the kingdom that his father once ruled. Chiron had one last piece of advice for him.
Always be kind to whomever you meet.
Farewell, Chiron!

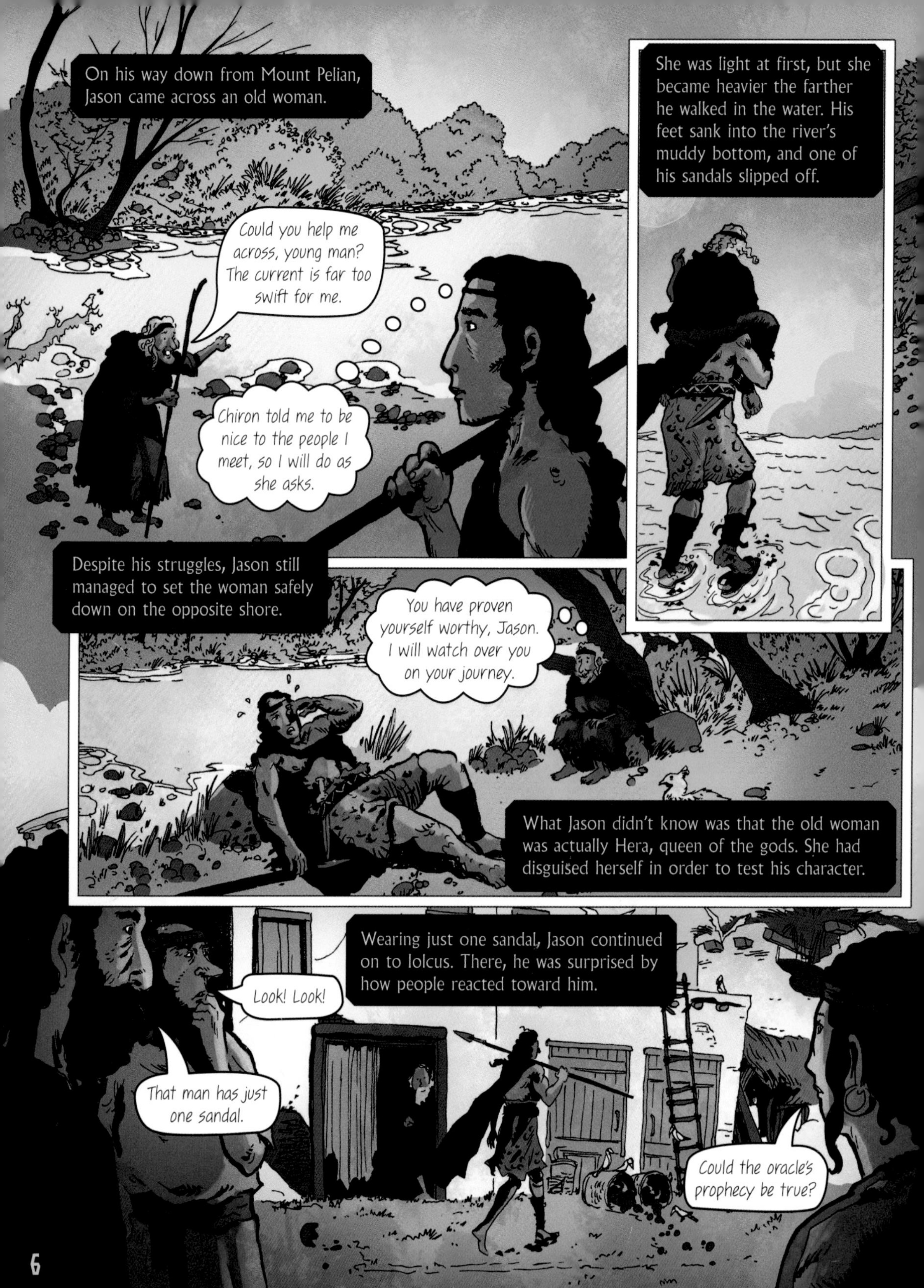
On his way down from Mount Pelian, Jason came across an old woman.
Could you help me across, young man? The current is far too swift for me.
Chiron told me to be nice to the people I meet, so I will do as she asks.
She was light at first, but she became heavier the farther he walked in the water. His feet sank into the river's muddy bottom, and one of his sandals slipped off.
Despite his struggles, Jason still managed to set the woman safely down on the opposite shore.
You have proven yourself worthy, Jason. I will watch over you on your journey.
What Jason didn't know was that the old woman was actually Hera, queen of the gods. She had disguised herself in order to test his character.
Wearing just one sandal, Jason continued on to Iolcus. There, he was surprised by how people reacted toward him.
Look! Look!
That man has just one sandal.
Could the oracle's prophecy be true?

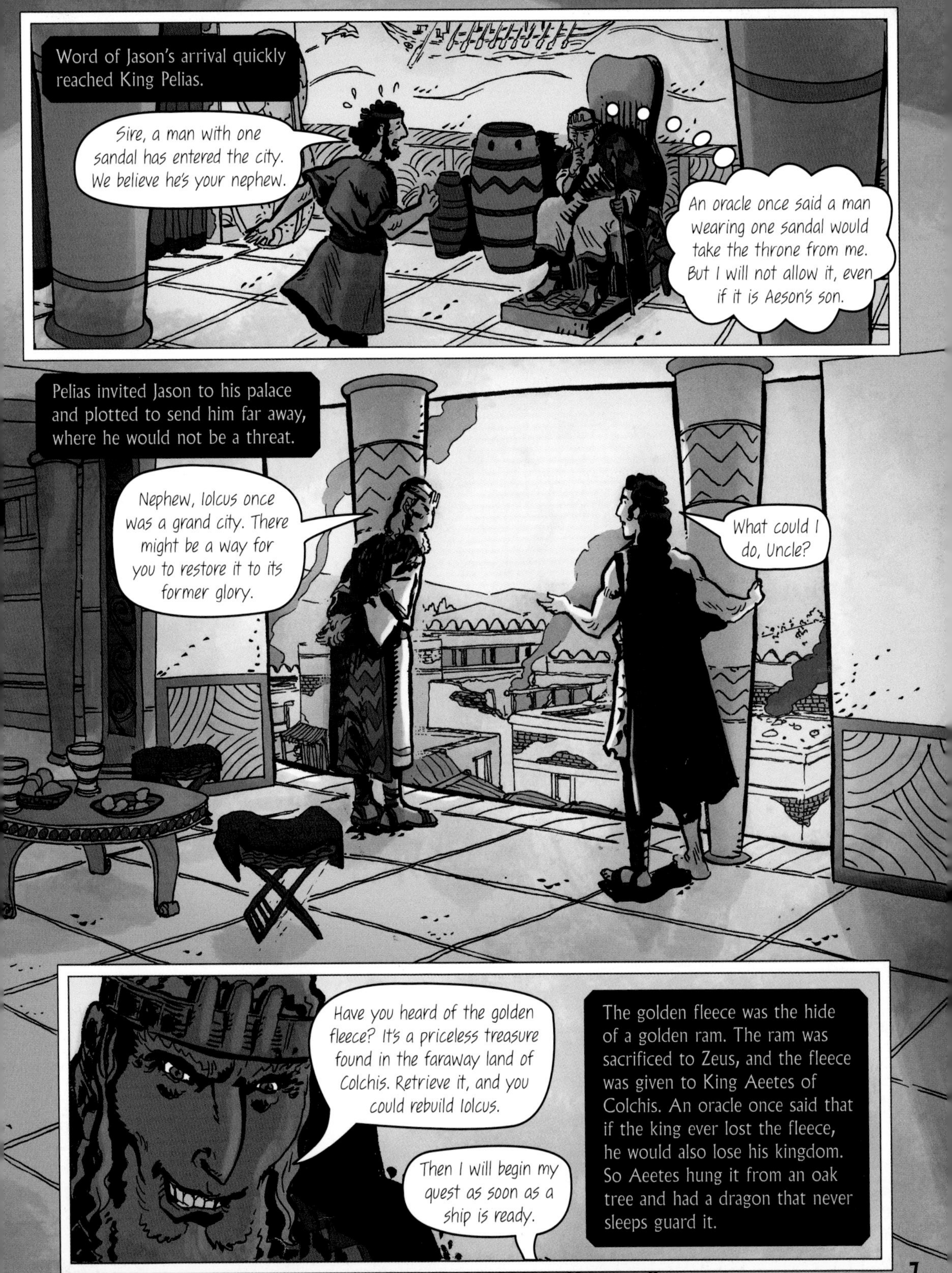
Word of Jason's arrival quickly reached King Pelias.
Sire, a man with one sandal has entered the city. We believe he's your nephew.
An oracle once said a man wearing one sandal would take the throne from me. But I will not allow it, even if it is Aeson's son.
Pelias invited Jason to his palace and plotted to send him far away, where he would not be a threat.
Nephew, Iolcus once was a grand city. There might be a way for you to restore it to its former glory.
What could I do, Uncle?
Have you heard of the golden fleece? It's a priceless treasure found in the faraway land of Colchis. Retrieve it, and you could rebuild Iolcus.
Then I will begin my quest as soon as a ship is ready.
The golden fleece was the hide of a golden ram. The ram was sacrificed to Zeus, and the fleece was given to King Aeetes of Colchis. An oracle once said that if the king ever lost the fleece, he would also lose his kingdom. So Aeetes hung it from an oak tree and had a dragon that never sleeps guard it.

CHAPTER TWO

THE ARGONAUTS

Because Jason had helped her cross the river, Hera watched over him. When he agreed to go on the quest to find the golden fleece, she sent Athena, the goddess of wisdom, to Iolcus. Athena guided the city's ship builder, Argus, in building the stoutest ship ever built—the *Argo*—for Jason's quest. Hera also called out for heroes to join Jason on his quest.

First came Orpheus, the best musician in the world. The trees swayed to his song as he plucked his lyre.

Even Hercules, the strongest man alive, heard of Jason's need for help.

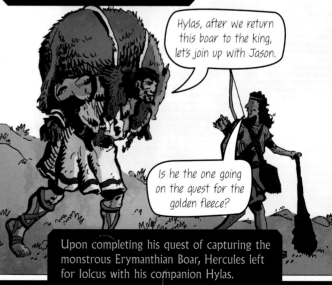

Hylas, after we return this boar to the king, let's join up with Jason.

Is he the one going on the quest for the golden fleece?

Upon completing his quest of capturing the monstrous Erymanthian Boar, Hercules left for Iolcus with his companion Hylas.

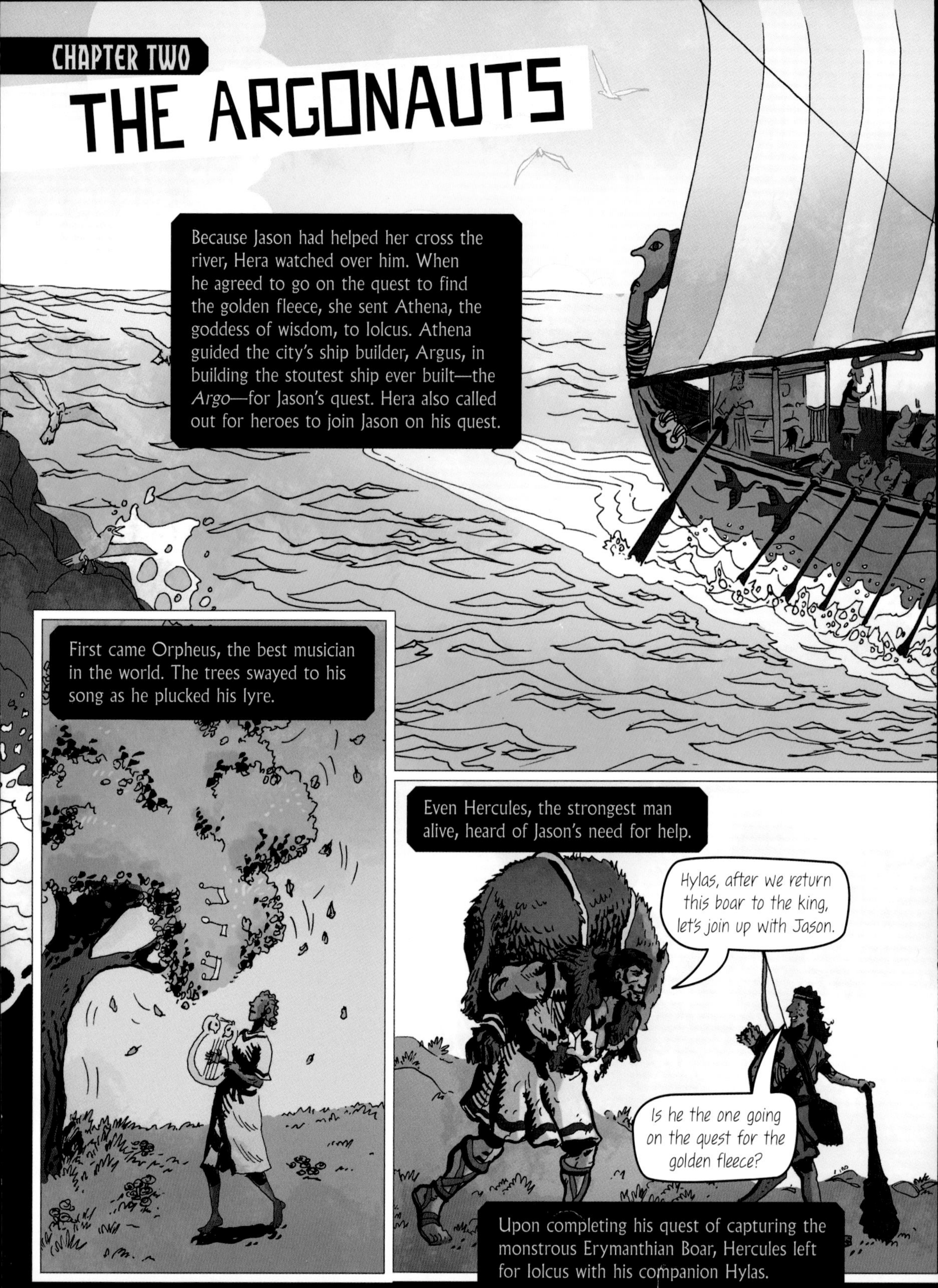

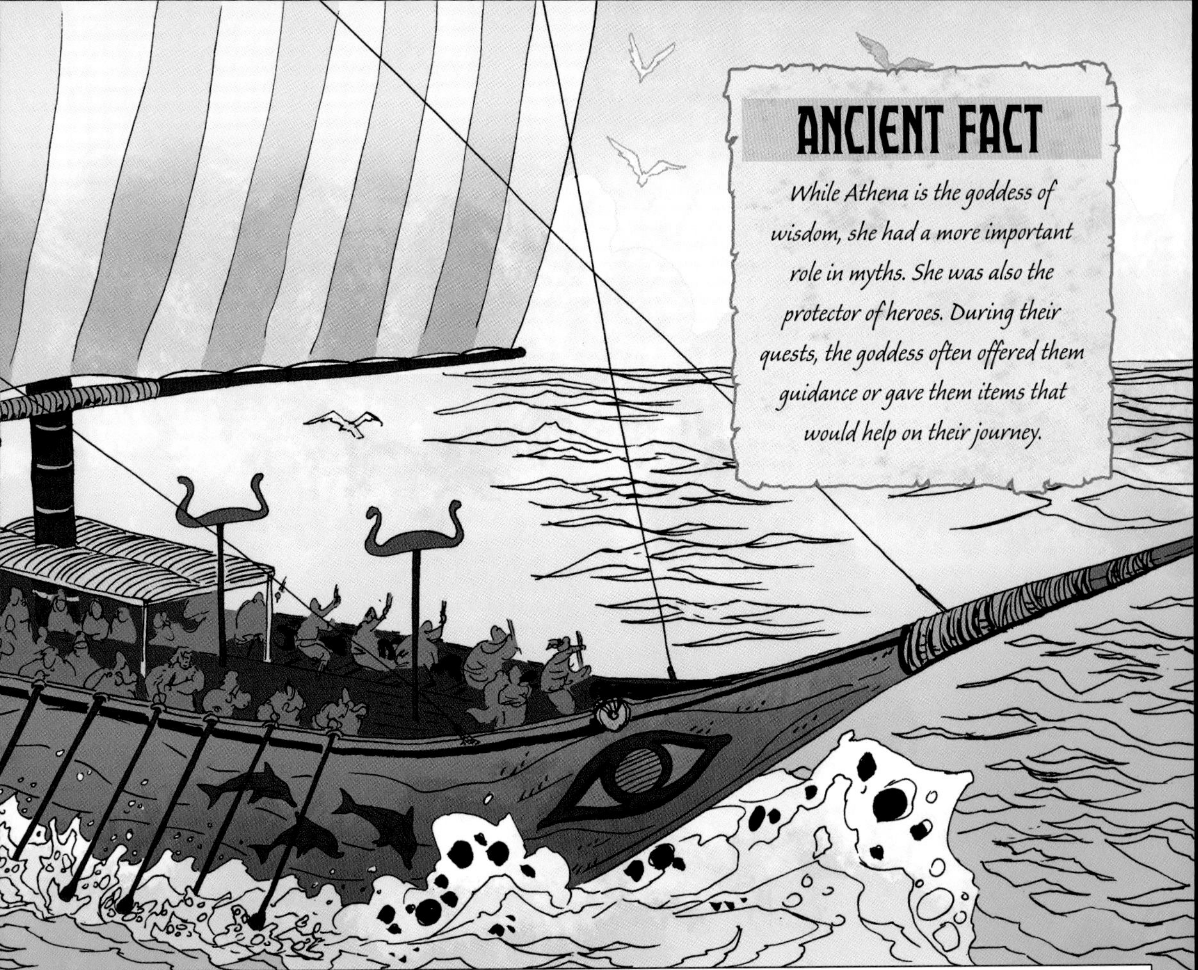

ANCIENT FACT

While Athena is the goddess of wisdom, she had a more important role in myths. She was also the protector of heroes. During their quests, the goddess often offered them guidance or gave them items that would help on their journey.

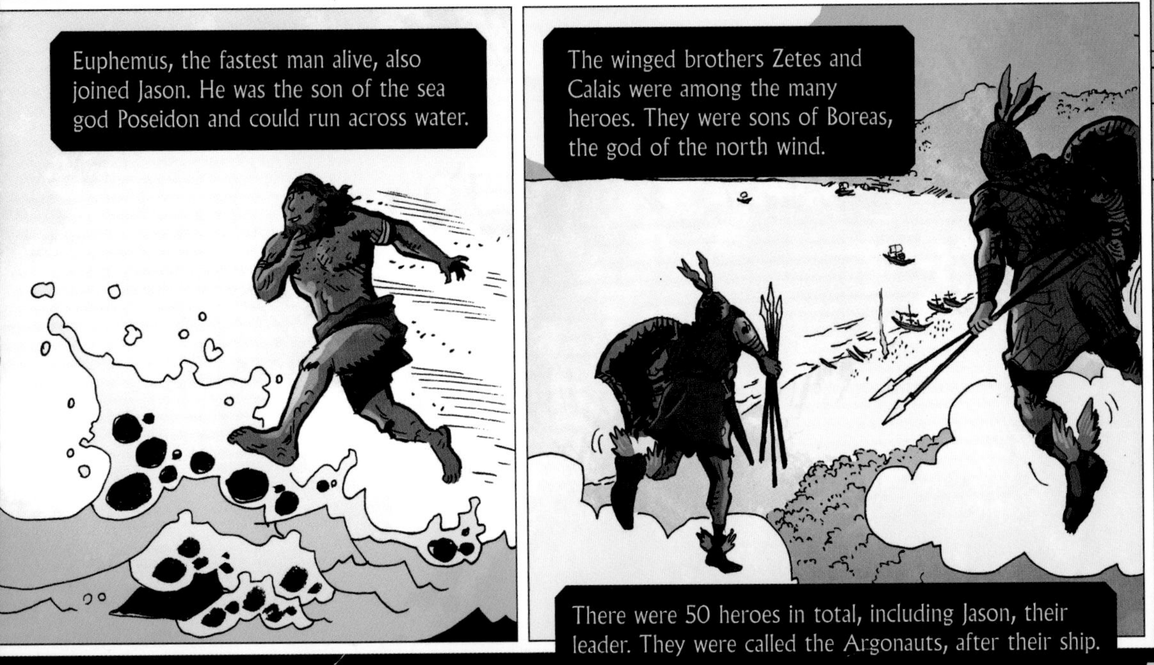
Euphemus, the fastest man alive, also joined Jason. He was the son of the sea god Poseidon and could run across water.
The winged brothers Zetes and Calais were among the many heroes. They were sons of Boreas, the god of the north wind.
There were 50 heroes in total, including Jason, their leader. They were called the Argonauts, after their ship.

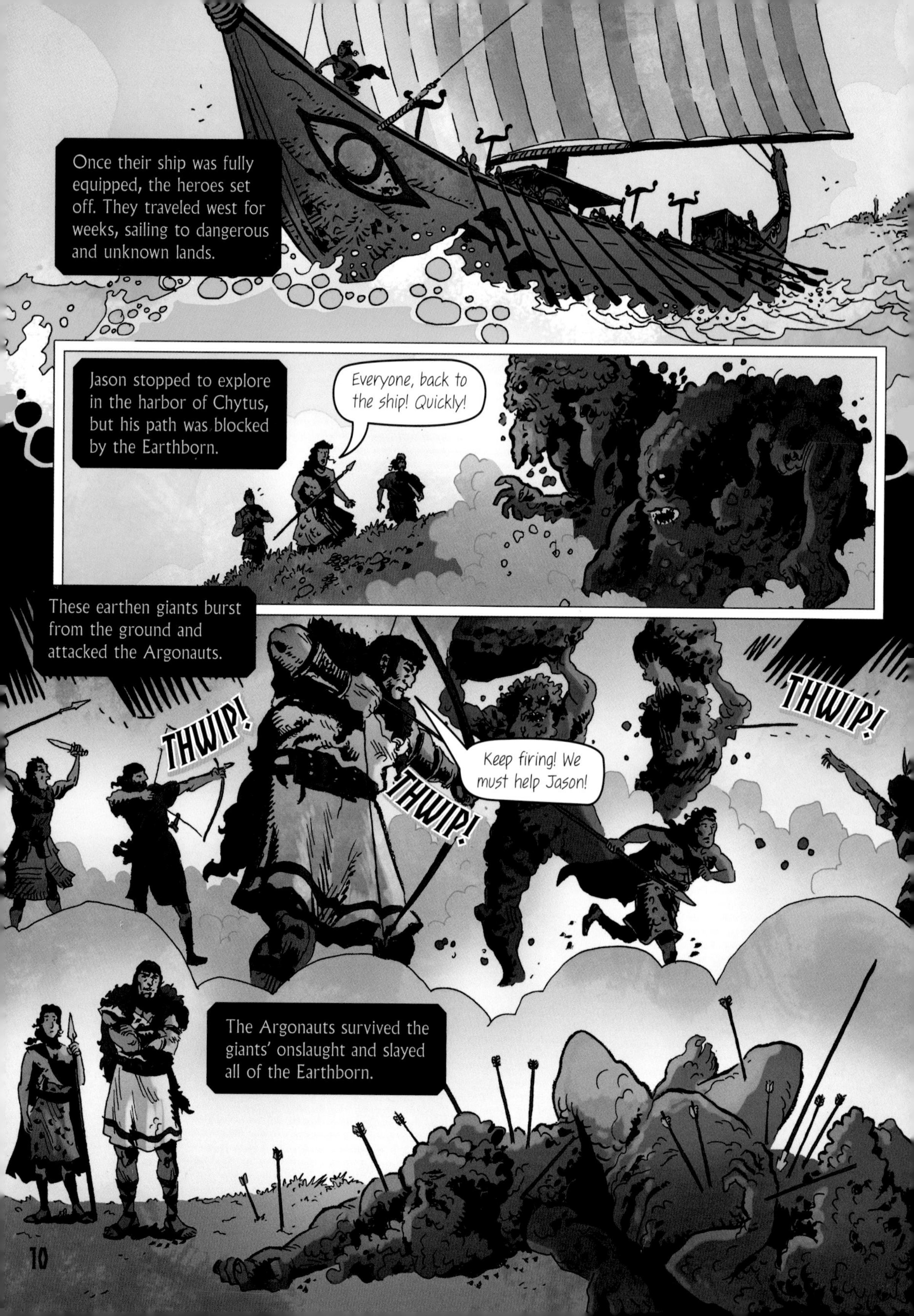
Once their ship was fully equipped, the heroes set off. They traveled west for weeks, sailing to dangerous and unknown lands.
Jason stopped to explore in the harbor of Chytus, but his path was blocked by the Earthborn.
Everyone, back to the ship! Quickly!
These earthen giants burst from the ground and attacked the Argonauts.
THWIP!
THWIP!
Keep firing! We must help Jason!
THWIP!
The Argonauts survived the giants' onslaught and slayed all of the Earthborn.

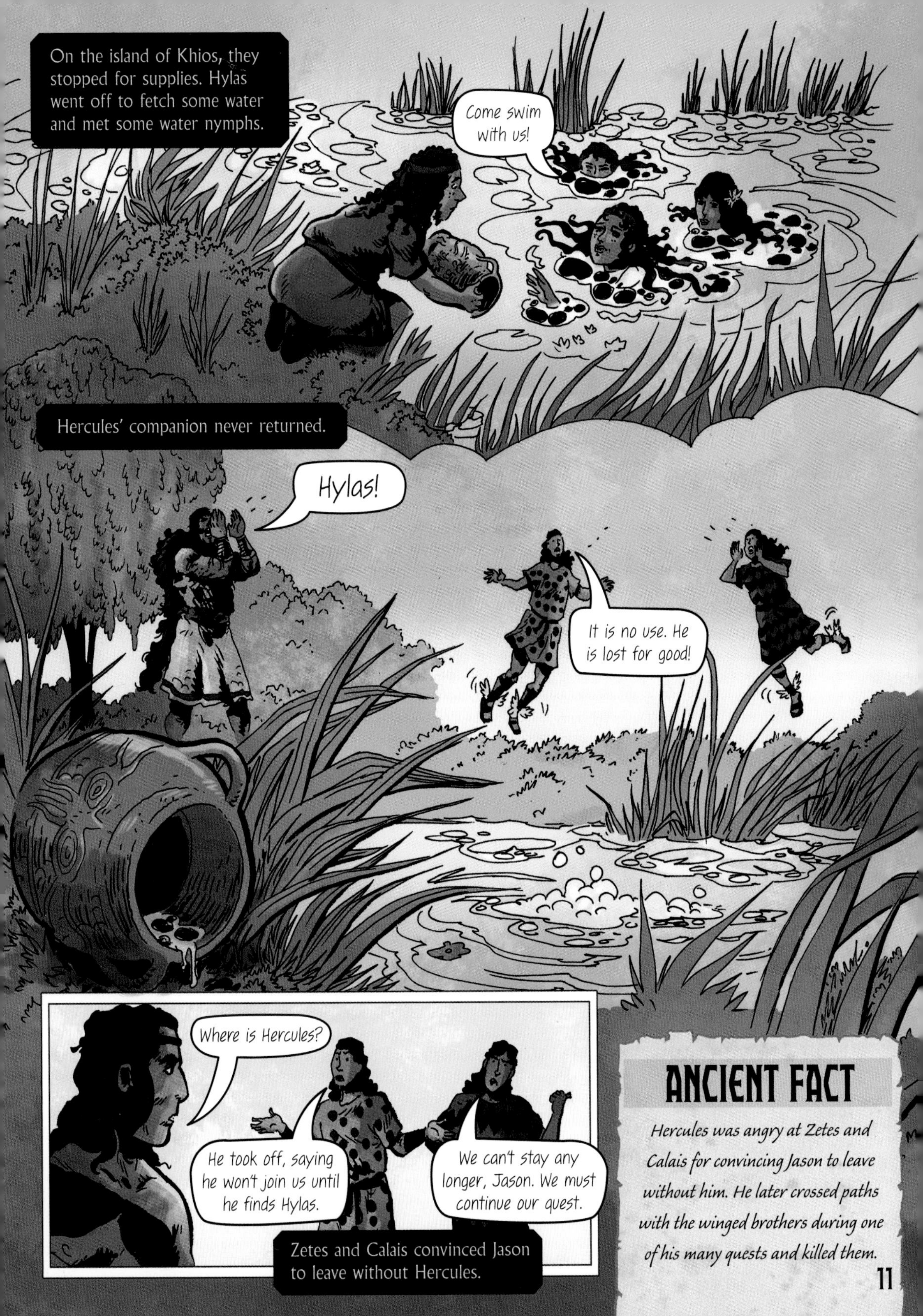
On the island of Khios, they stopped for supplies. Hylas went off to fetch some water and met some water nymphs.
Come swim with us!
Hercules' companion never returned.
Hylas!
It is no use. He is lost for good!
Where is Hercules?
He took off, saying he won't join us until he finds Hylas.
We can't stay any longer, Jason. We must continue our quest.
Zetes and Calais convinced Jason to leave without Hercules.

ANCIENT FACT

Hercules was angry at Zetes and Calais for convincing Jason to leave without him. He later crossed paths with the winged brothers during one of his many quests and killed them.

CHAPTER THREE

KING PHINEUS

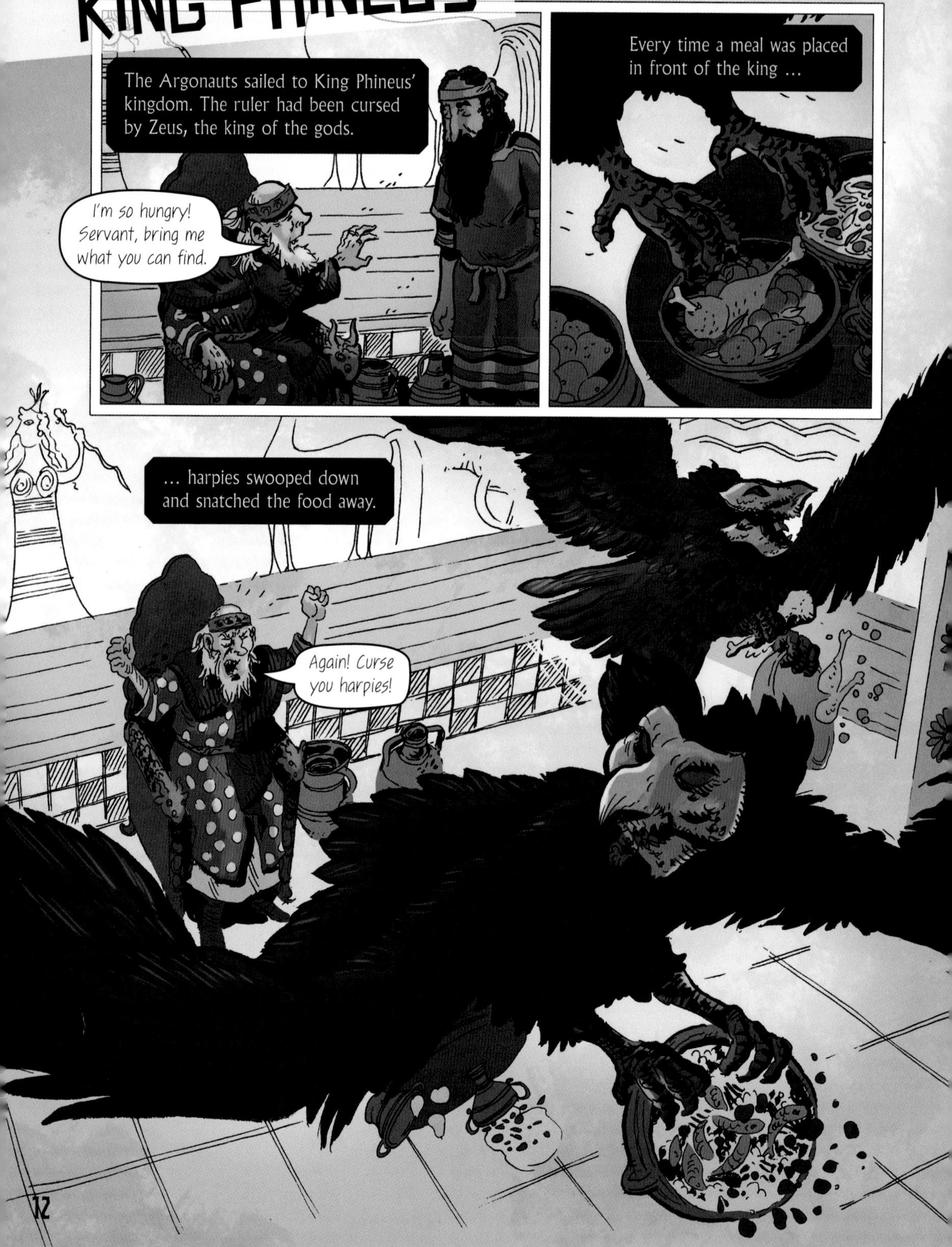

The Argonauts sailed to King Phineus' kingdom. The ruler had been cursed by Zeus, the king of the gods.
I'm so hungry! Servant, bring me what you can find.
Every time a meal was placed in front of the king ...
... harpies swooped down and snatched the food away.
Again! Curse you harpies!

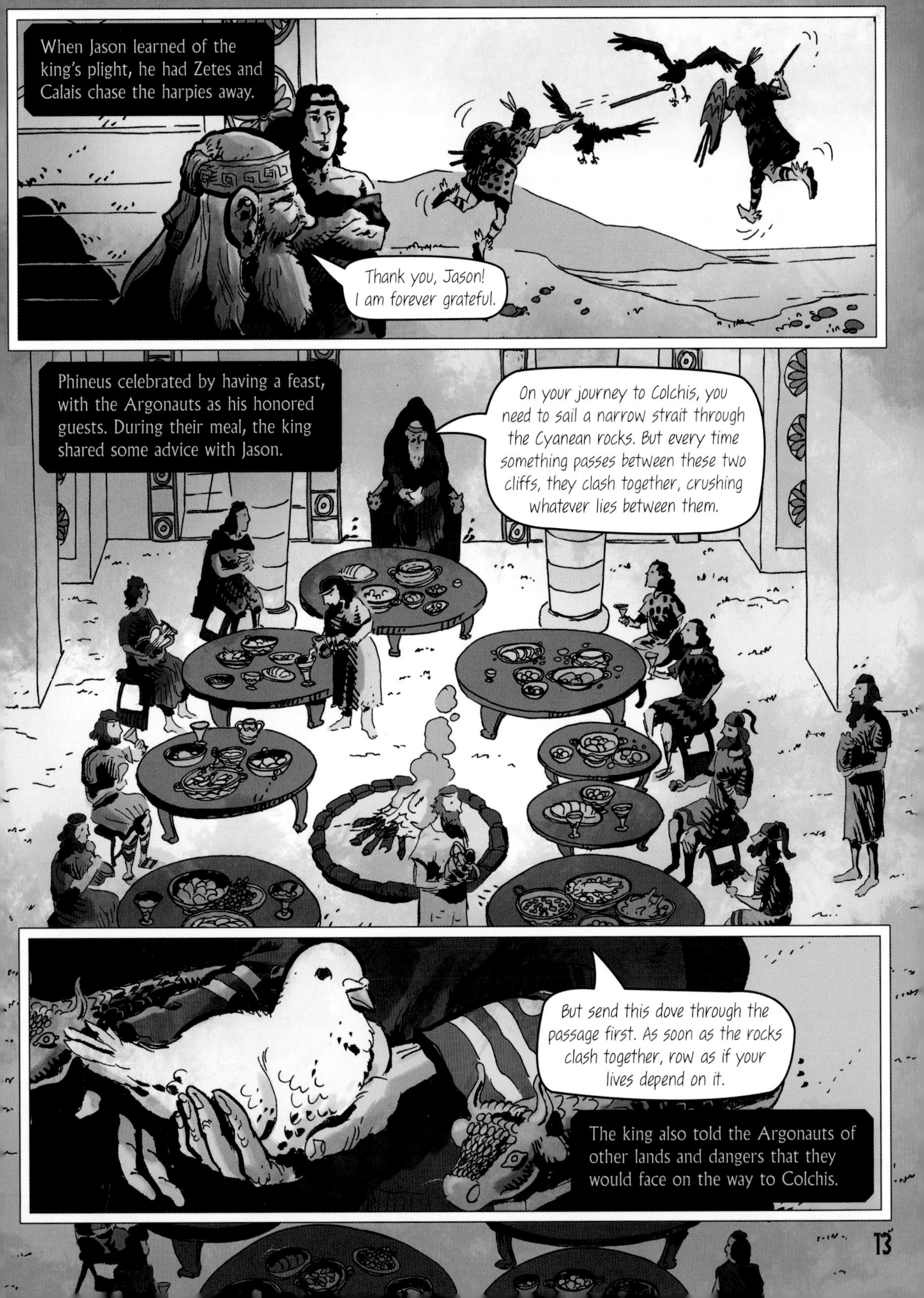
When Jason learned of the king's plight, he had Zetes and Calais chase the harpies away.
Thank you, Jason! I am forever grateful.
Phineus celebrated by having a feast, with the Argonauts as his honored guests. During their meal, the king shared some advice with Jason.
On your journey to Colchis, you need to sail a narrow strait through the Cyanean rocks. But every time something passes between these two cliffs, they clash together, crushing whatever lies between them.
But send this dove through the passage first. As soon as the rocks clash together, row as if your lives depend on it.
The king also told the Argonauts of other lands and dangers that they would face on the way to Colchis.

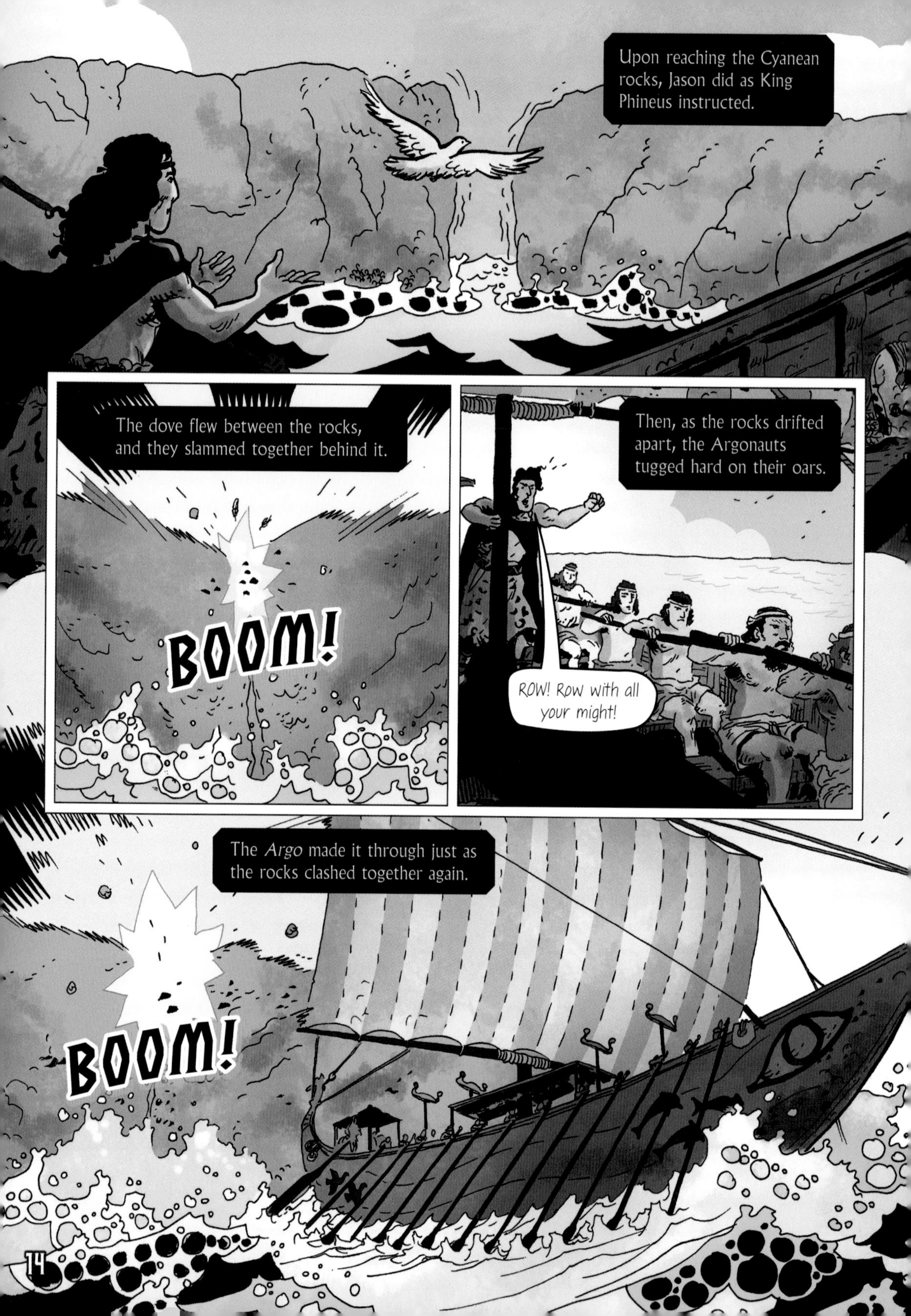
Upon reaching the Cyanean rocks, Jason did as King Phineus instructed.
The dove flew between the rocks, and they slammed together behind it.
BOOM!
Then, as the rocks drifted apart, the Argonauts tugged hard on their oars.
ROW! Row with all your might!
The *Argo* made it through just as the rocks clashed together again.
BOOM!

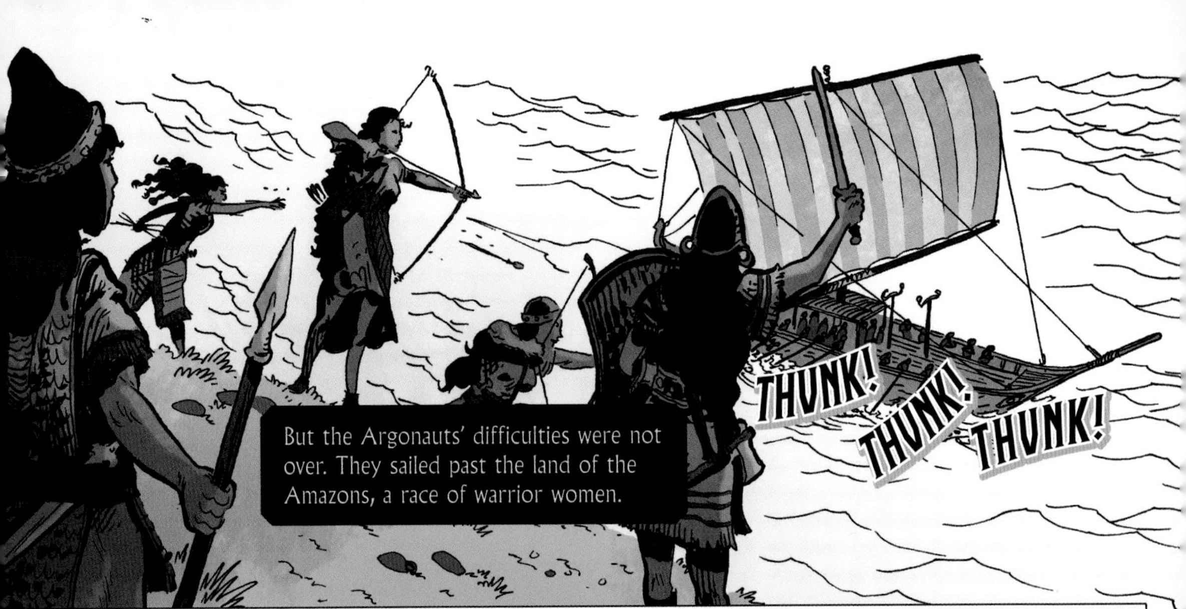
But the Argonauts' difficulties were not over. They sailed past the land of the Amazons, a race of warrior women.
THUNK!
THUNK!
THUNK!

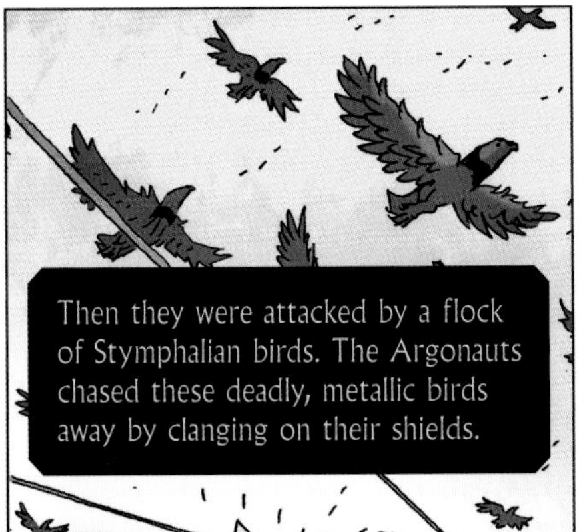
Then they were attacked by a flock of Stymphalian birds. The Argonauts chased these deadly, metallic birds away by clanging on their shields.
CLANG!

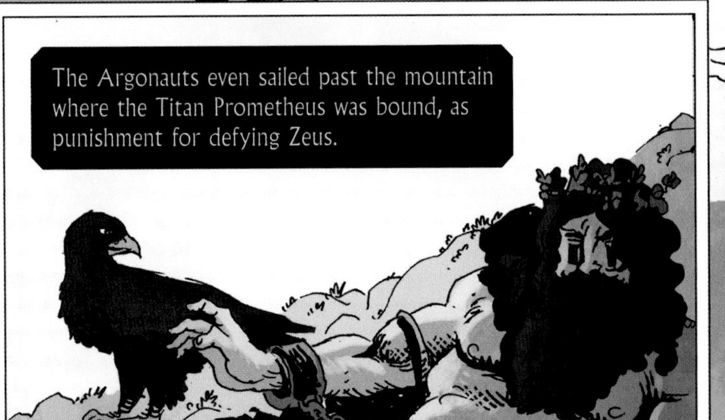
The Argonauts even sailed past the mountain where the Titan Prometheus was bound, as punishment for defying Zeus.

ANCIENT FACT

In Greek myths, Prometheus gave people fire. Angered at the Titan's actions, Zeus punished Prometheus by chaining him to the side of a mountain. Every day an eagle would come and pluck out Prometheus' liver. But because he was immortal, his liver would grow back every night.

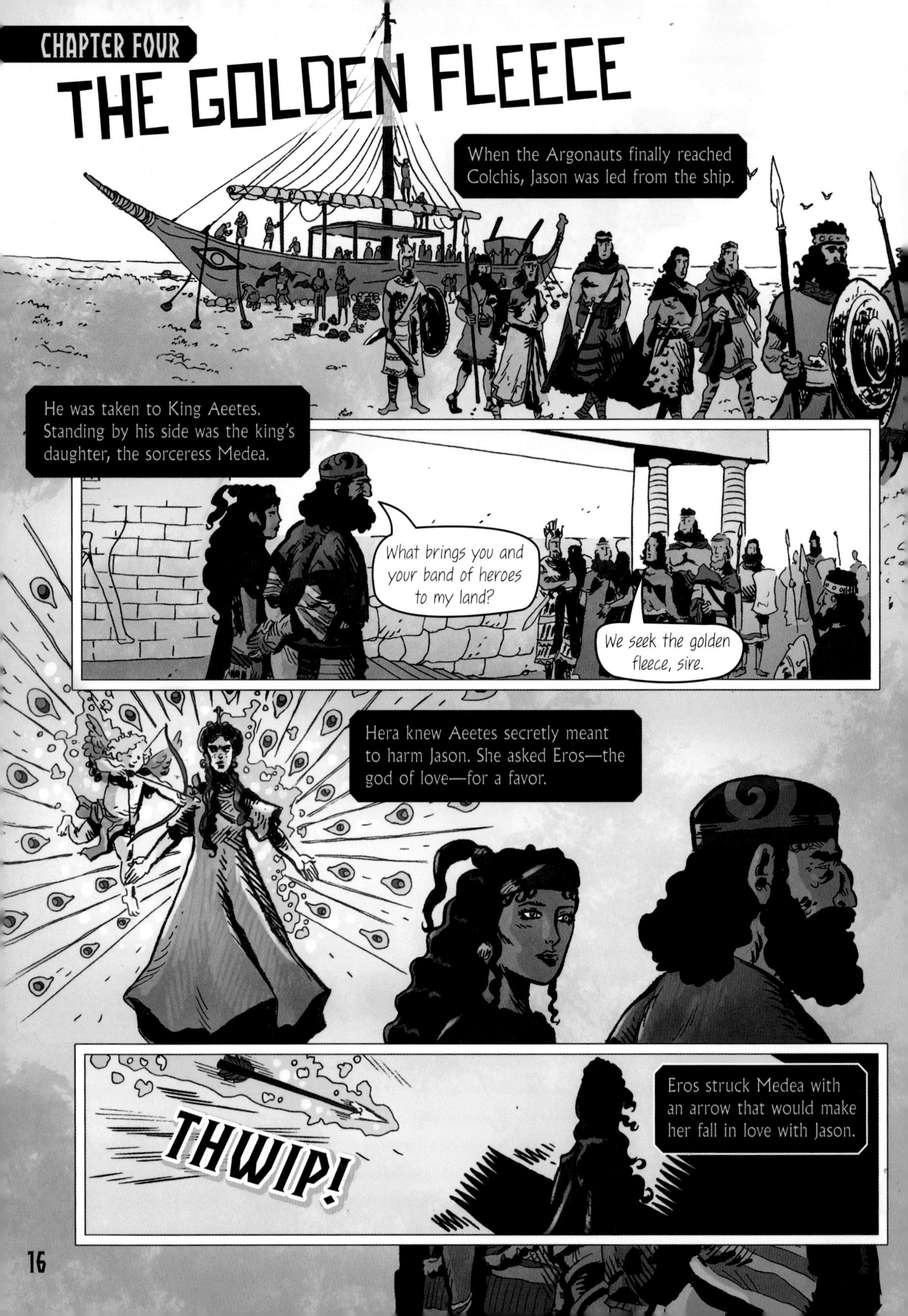
CHAPTER FOUR
THE GOLDEN FLEECE
When the Argonauts finally reached Colchis, Jason was led from the ship.
He was taken to King Aeetes. Standing by his side was the king's daughter, the sorceress Medea.
What brings you and your band of heroes to my land?
We seek the golden fleece, sire.
Hera knew Aeetes secretly meant to harm Jason. She asked Eros—the god of love—for a favor.
THWIP!
Eros struck Medea with an arrow that would make her fall in love with Jason.

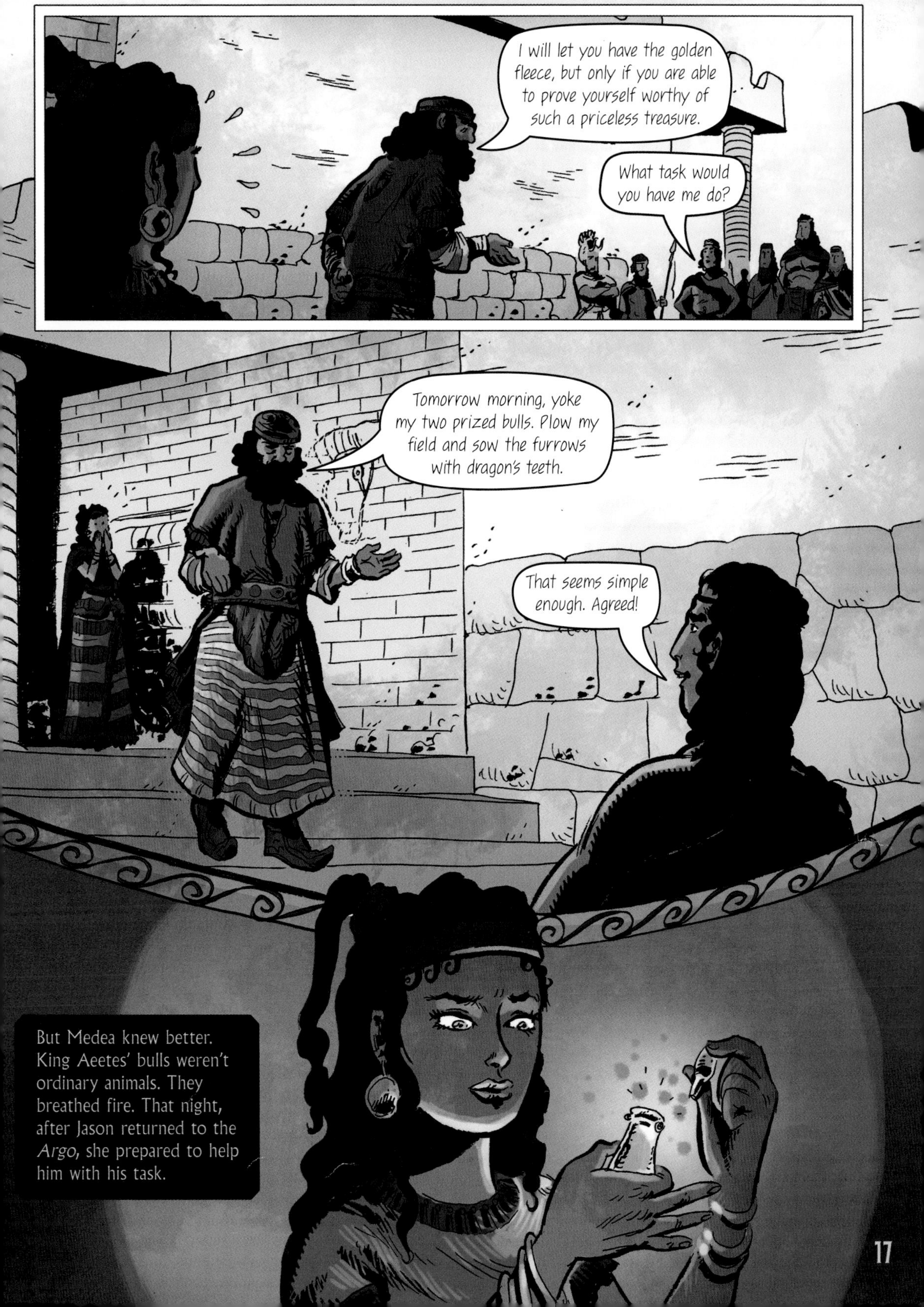

I will let you have the golden fleece, but only if you are able to prove yourself worthy of such a priceless treasure.
What task would you have me do?
Tomorrow morning, yoke my two prized bulls. Plow my field and sow the furrows with dragon's teeth.
That seems simple enough. Agreed!
But Medea knew better. King Aeetes' bulls weren't ordinary animals. They breathed fire. That night, after Jason returned to the *Argo*, she prepared to help him with his task.

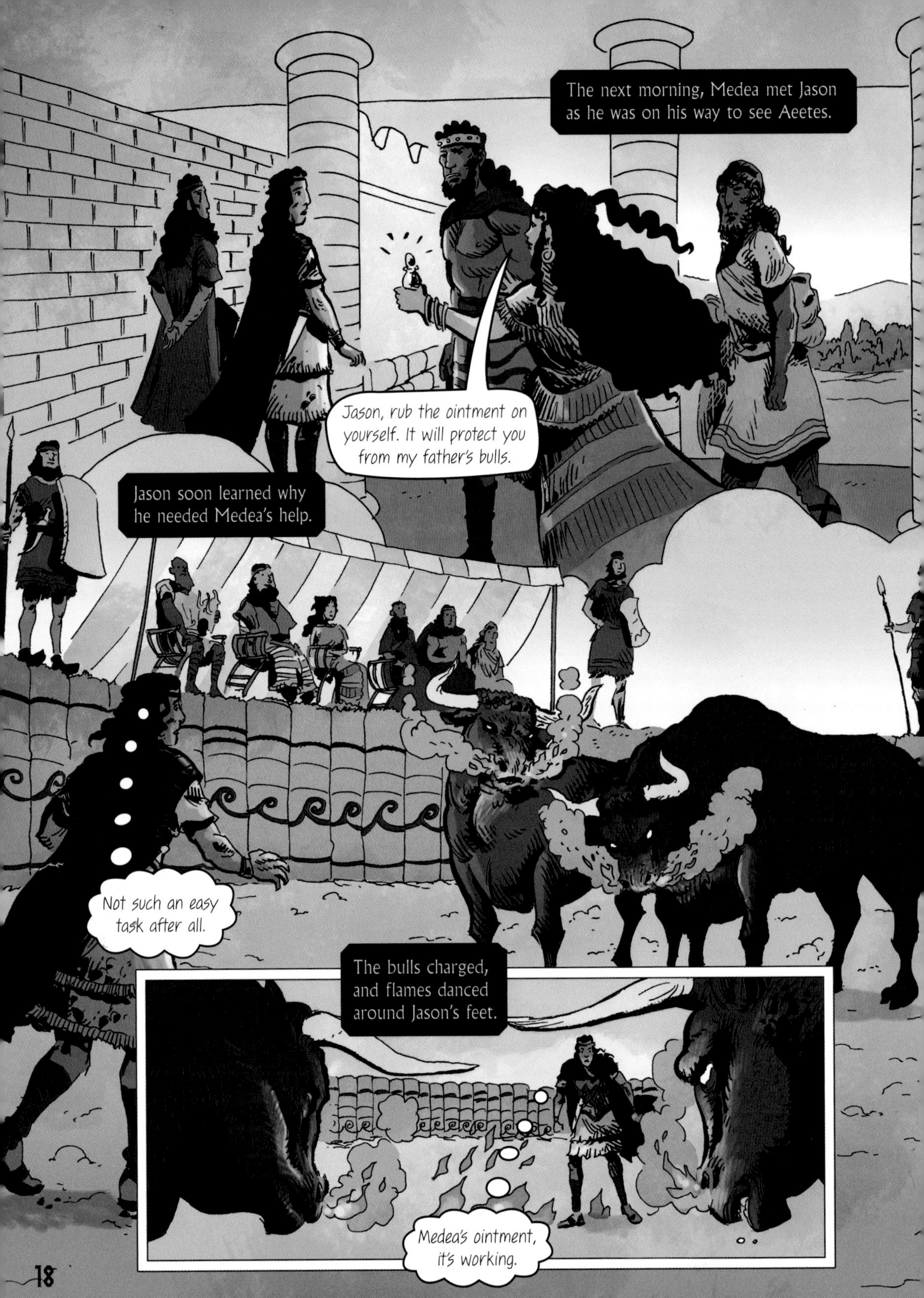

The next morning, Medea met Jason as he was on his way to see Aeetes.
Jason, rub the ointment on yourself. It will protect you from my father's bulls.
Jason soon learned why he needed Medea's help.
Not such an easy task after all.
The bulls charged, and flames danced around Jason's feet.
Medea's ointment, it's working.

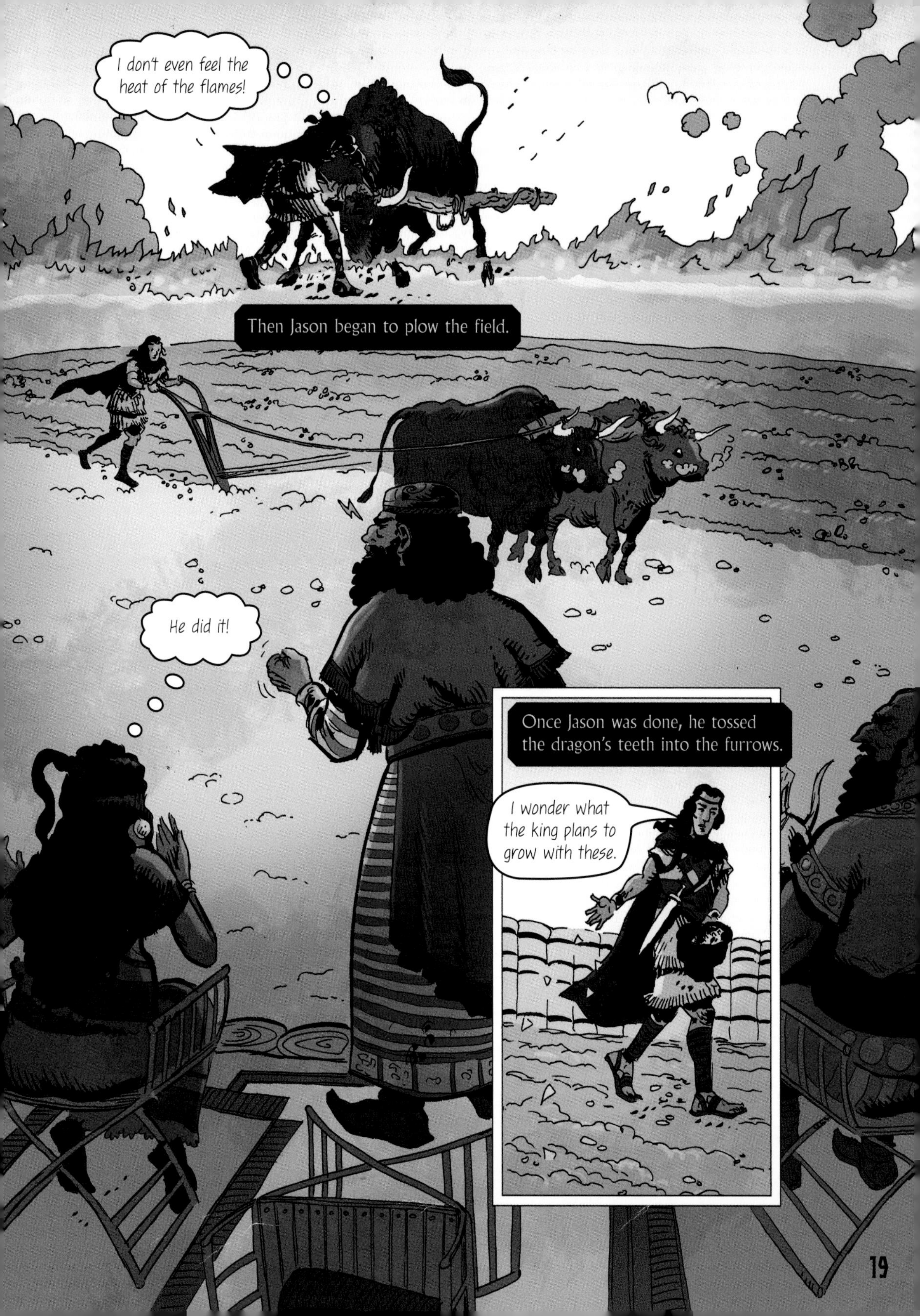
I don't even feel the heat of the flames!
Then Jason began to plow the field.
He did it!
Once Jason was done, he tossed the dragon's teeth into the furrows.
I wonder what the king plans to grow with these.

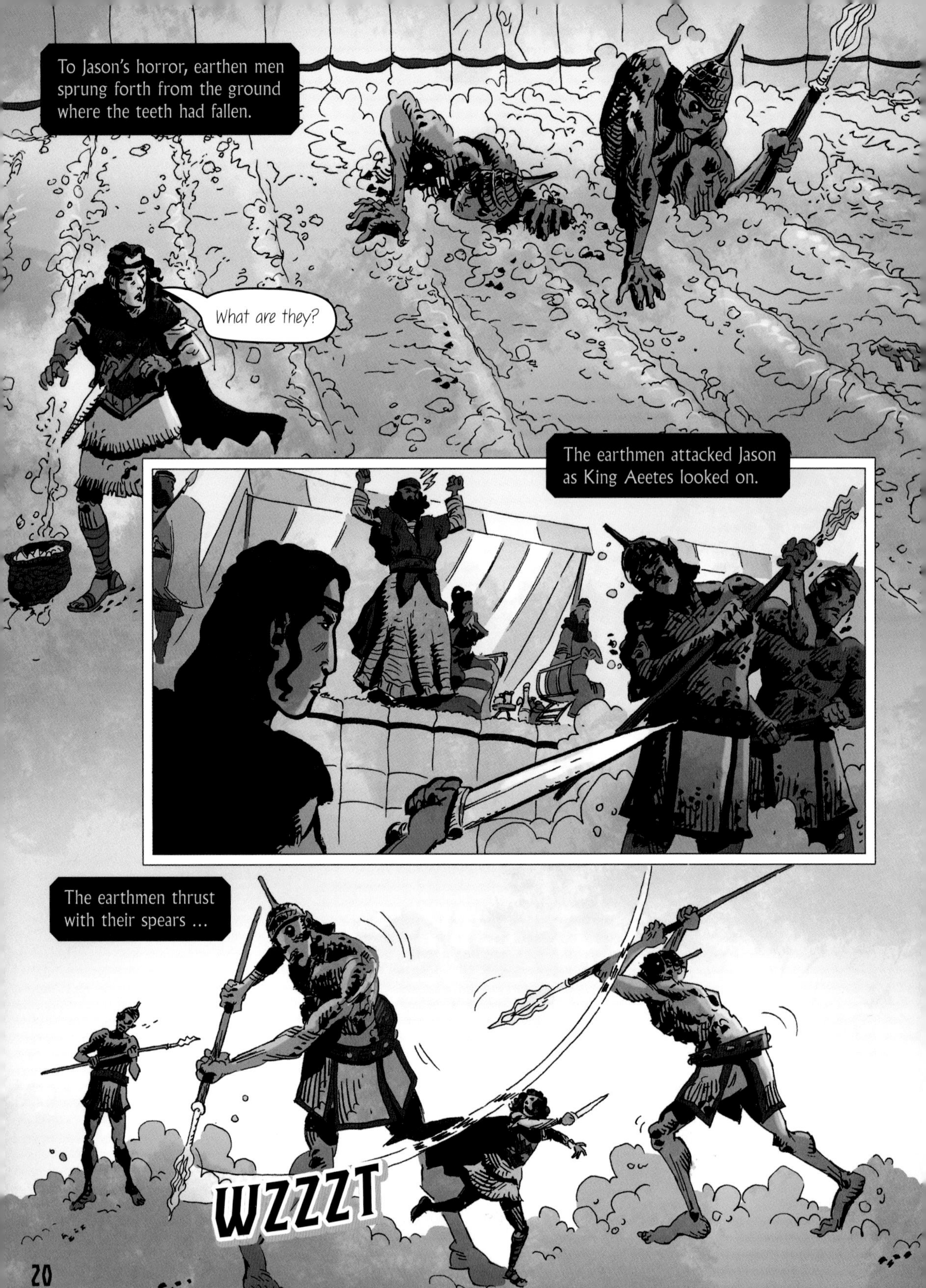
To Jason's horror, earthen men sprung forth from the ground where the teeth had fallen.
What are they?
The earthmen attacked Jason as King Aeetes looked on.
The earthmen thrust with their spears ...
WZZZT

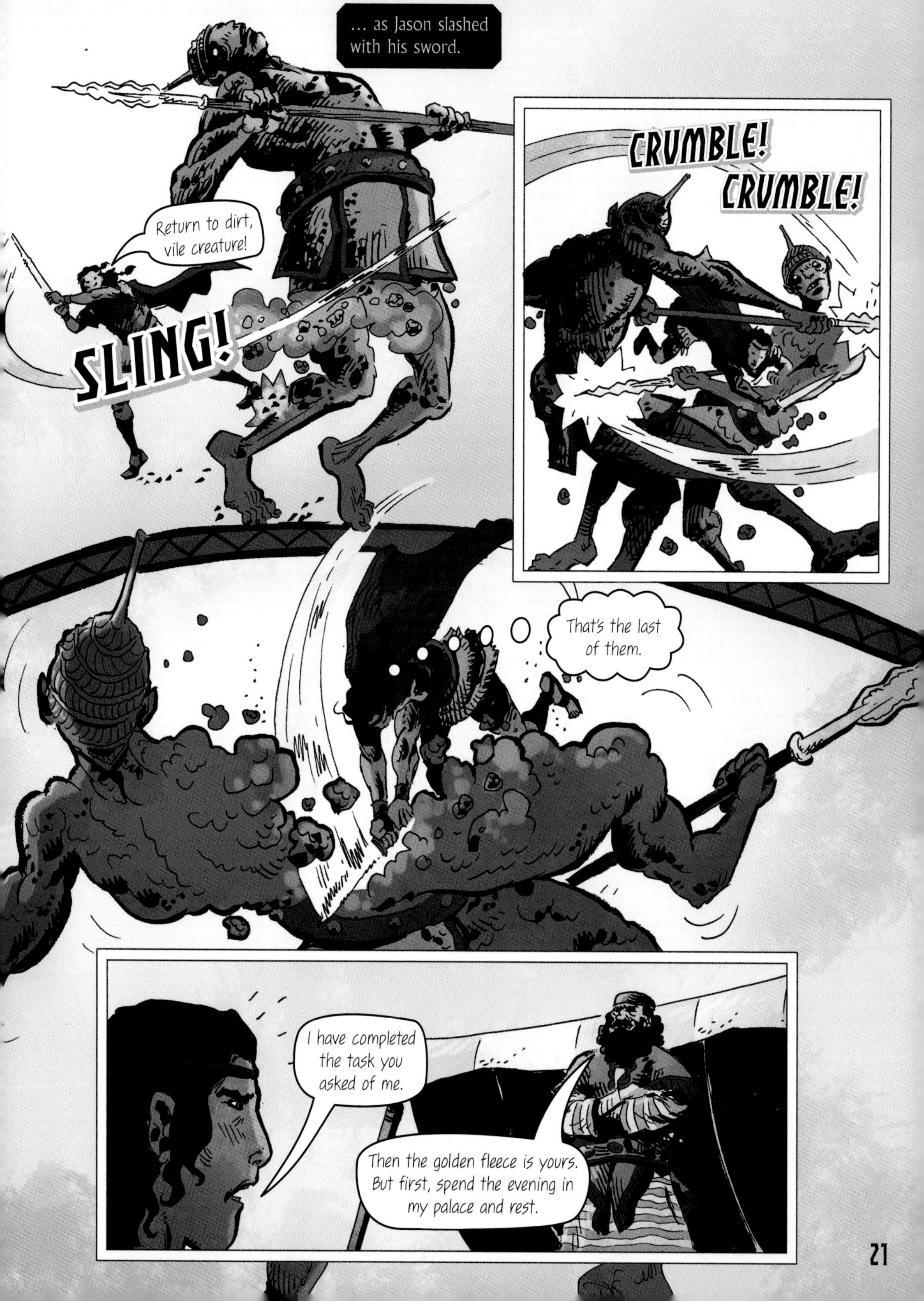
... as Jason slashed with his sword.
Return to dirt, vile creature!
SLING!
CRUMBLE! CRUMBLE!
That's the last of them.
I have completed the task you asked of me.
Then the golden fleece is yours. But first, spend the evening in my palace and rest.

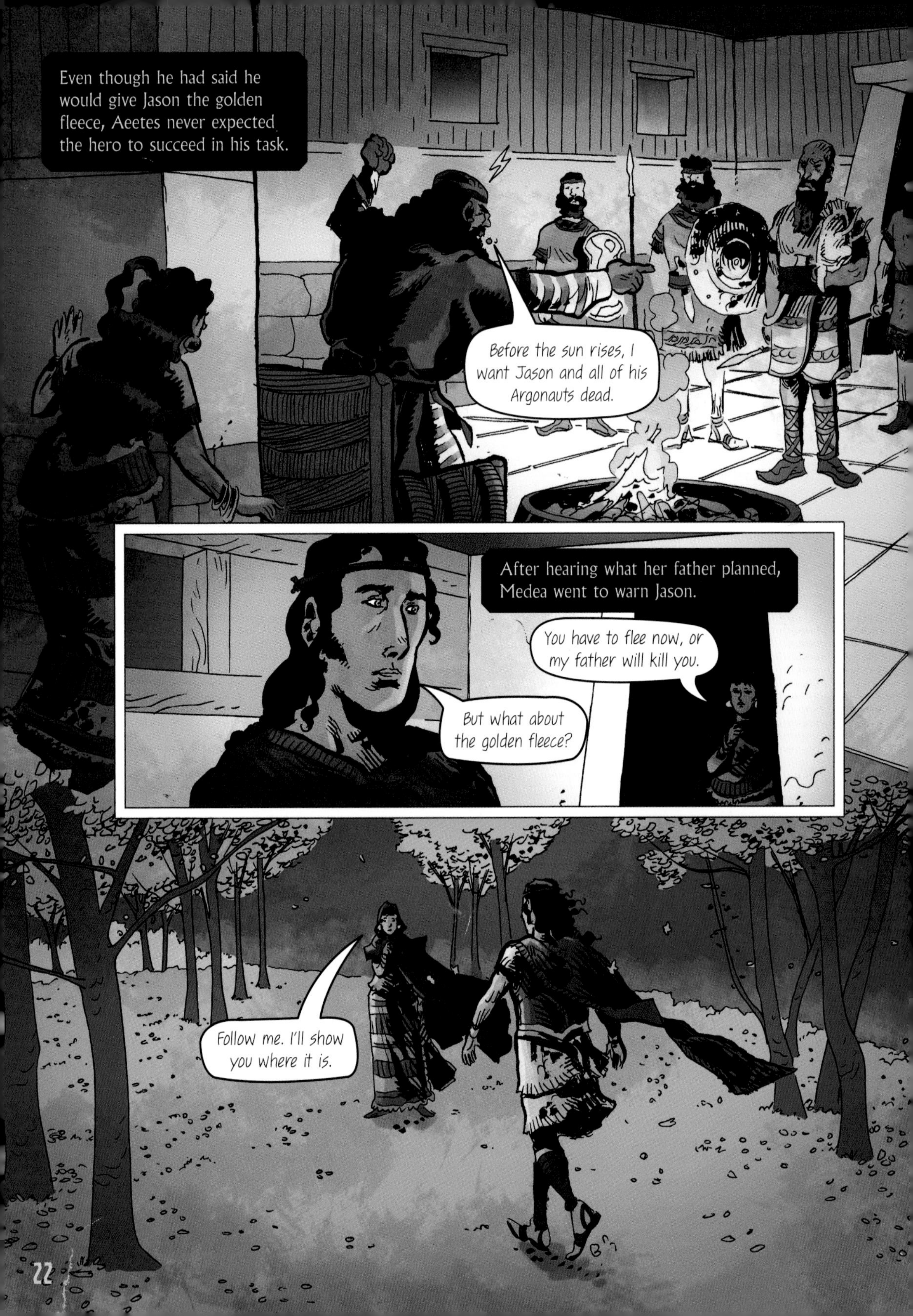
Even though he had said he would give Jason the golden fleece, Aeetes never expected the hero to succeed in his task.
Before the sun rises, I want Jason and all of his Argonauts dead.
After hearing what her father planned, Medea went to warn Jason.
You have to flee now, or my father will kill you.
But what about the golden fleece?
Follow me. I'll show you where it is.

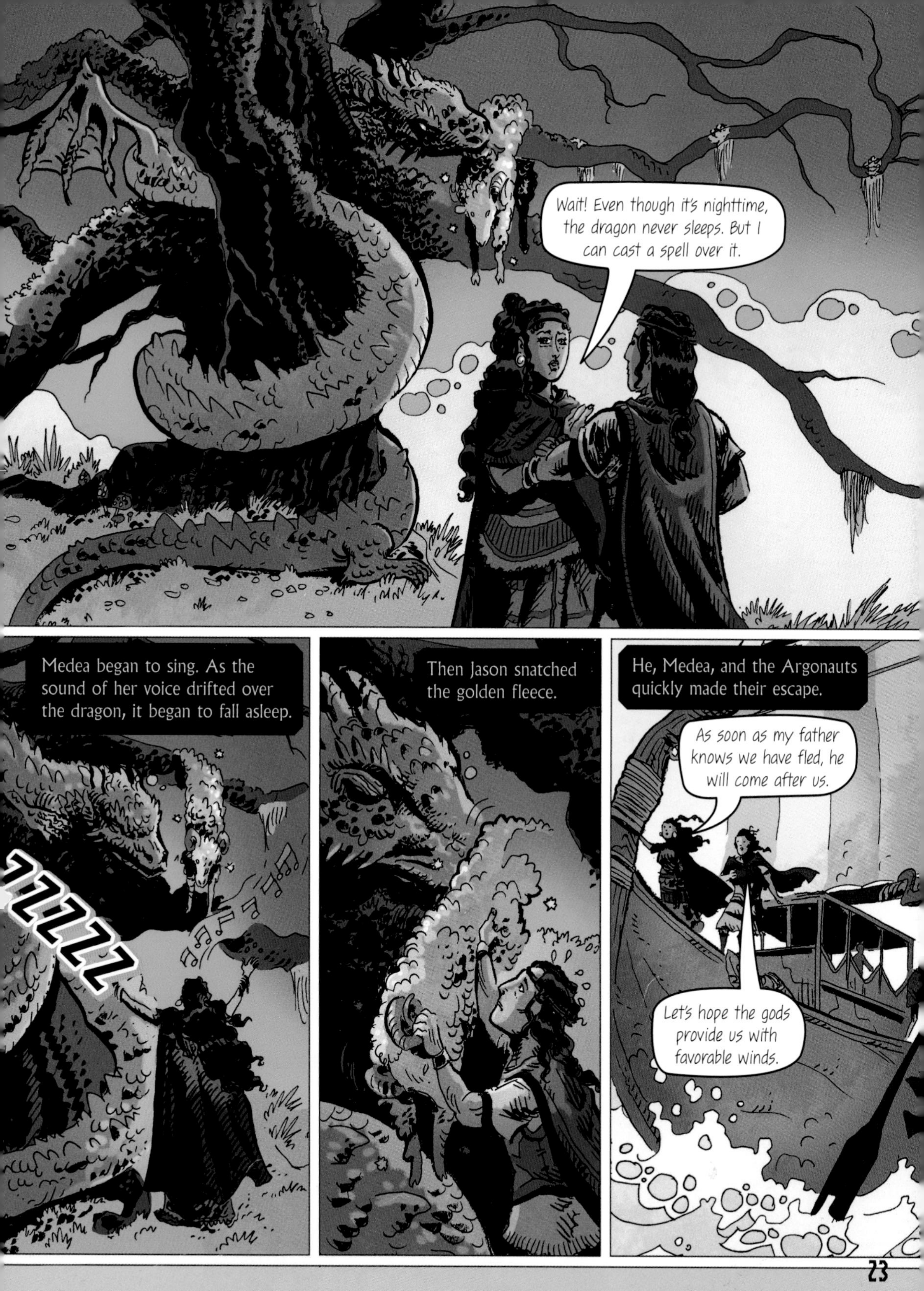

Wait! Even though it's nighttime, the dragon never sleeps. But I can cast a spell over it.
Medea began to sing. As the sound of her voice drifted over the dragon, it began to fall asleep.
ZZZZZ
Then Jason snatched the golden fleece.
He, Medea, and the Argonauts quickly made their escape.
As soon as my father knows we have fled, he will come after us.
Let's hope the gods provide us with favorable winds.

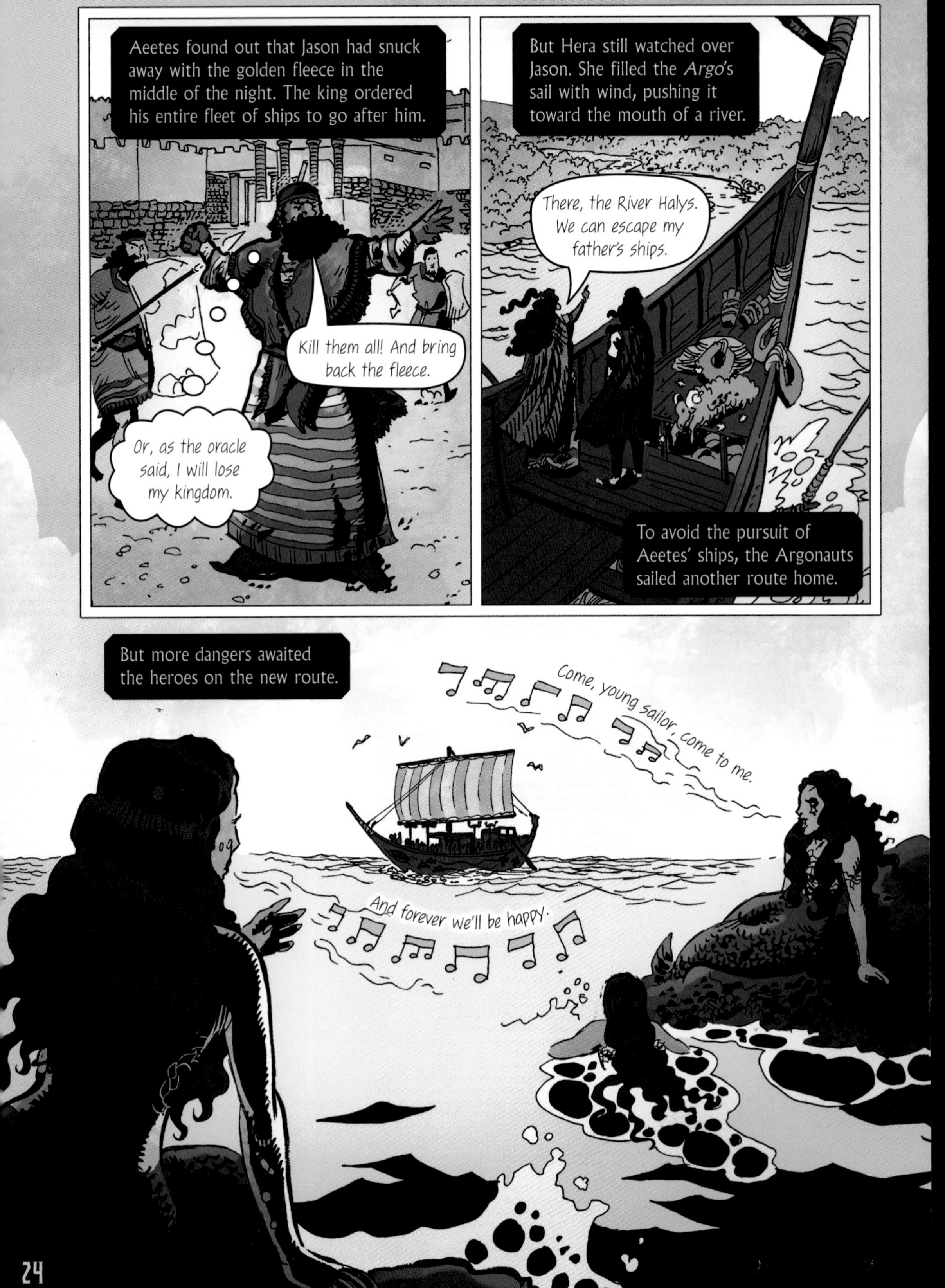

Aeetes found out that Jason had snuck away with the golden fleece in the middle of the night. The king ordered his entire fleet of ships to go after him.
Kill them all! And bring back the fleece.
Or, as the oracle said, I will lose my kingdom.
But Hera still watched over Jason. She filled the *Argo*'s sail with wind, pushing it toward the mouth of a river.
There, the River Halys. We can escape my father's ships.
To avoid the pursuit of Aeetes' ships, the Argonauts sailed another route home.
But more dangers awaited the heroes on the new route.
Come, young sailor, come to me.
And forever we'll be happy.

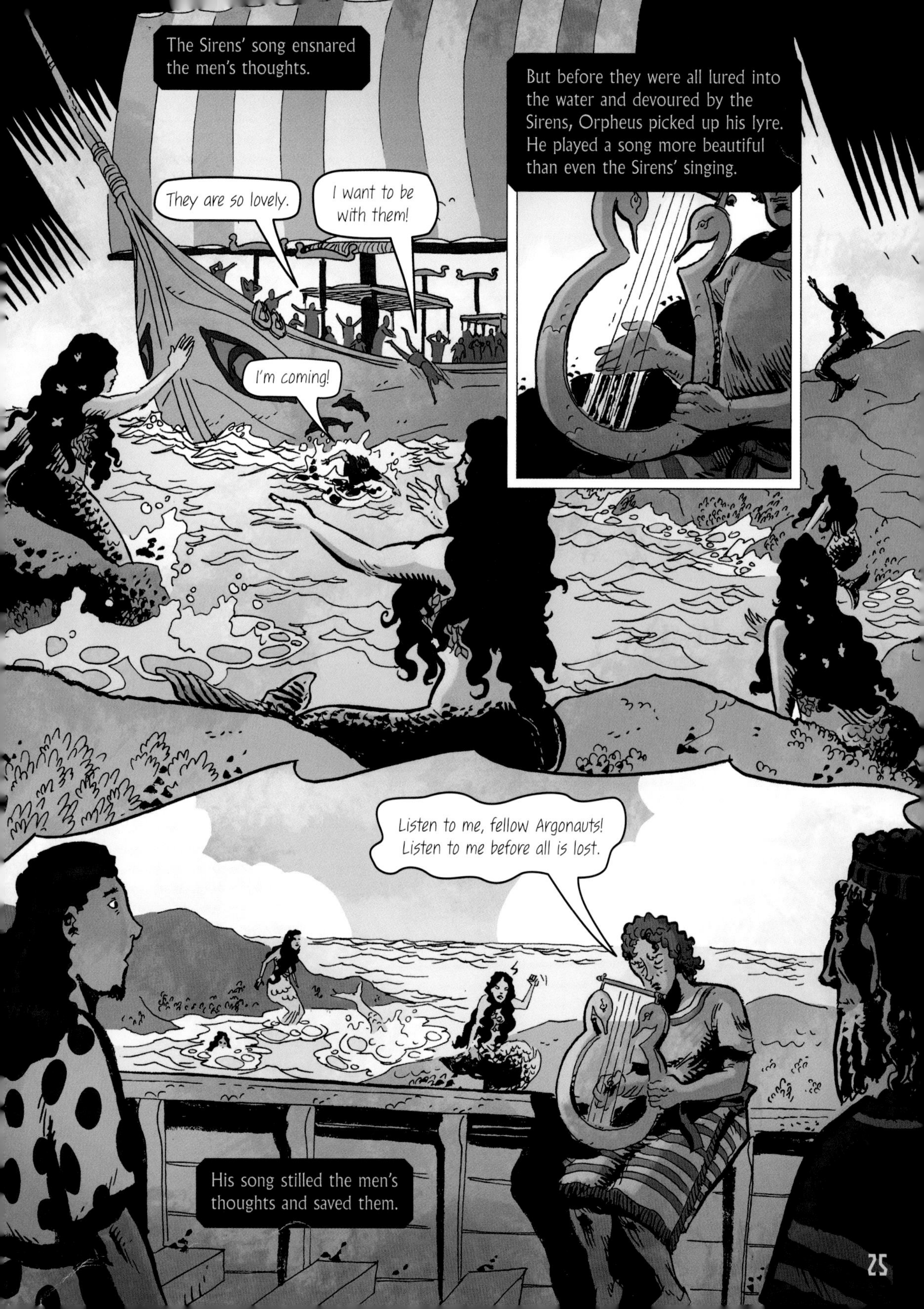
The Sirens' song ensnared the men's thoughts.
They are so lovely.
I want to be with them!
I'm coming!
But before they were all lured into the water and devoured by the Sirens, Orpheus picked up his lyre. He played a song more beautiful than even the Sirens' singing.
Listen to me, fellow Argonauts! Listen to me before all is lost.
His song stilled the men's thoughts and saved them.

CHAPTER FIVE
JASON'S JOURNEY HOME

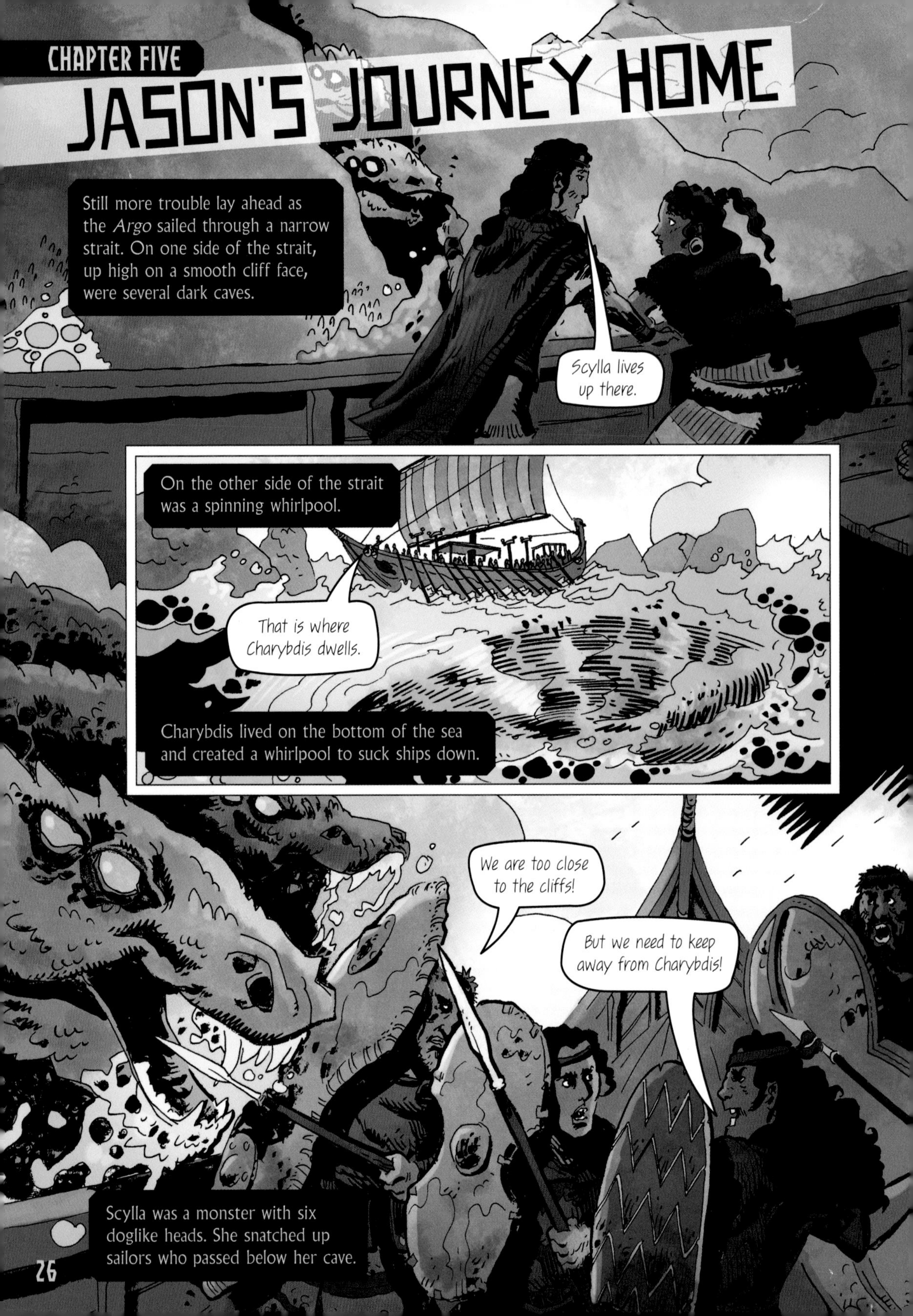
Still more trouble lay ahead as the *Argo* sailed through a narrow strait. On one side of the strait, up high on a smooth cliff face, were several dark caves.
Scylla lives up there.
On the other side of the strait was a spinning whirlpool.
That is where Charybdis dwells.
Charybdis lived on the bottom of the sea and created a whirlpool to suck ships down.
We are too close to the cliffs!
But we need to keep away from Charybdis!
Scylla was a monster with six doglike heads. She snatched up sailors who passed below her cave.

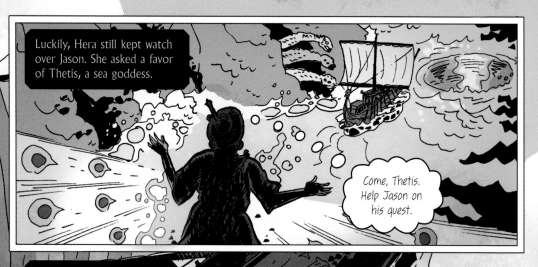

Luckily, Hera still kept watch over Jason. She asked a favor of Thetis, a sea goddess.

Come, Thetis. Help Jason on his quest.

Thetis sent Nereids—sea nymphs—to help the *Argo*.

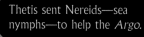

They lifted the *Argo* above the roiling waters of Charybdis ...

Look! Look!

We're saved!

... and carried the ship safely through the strait.

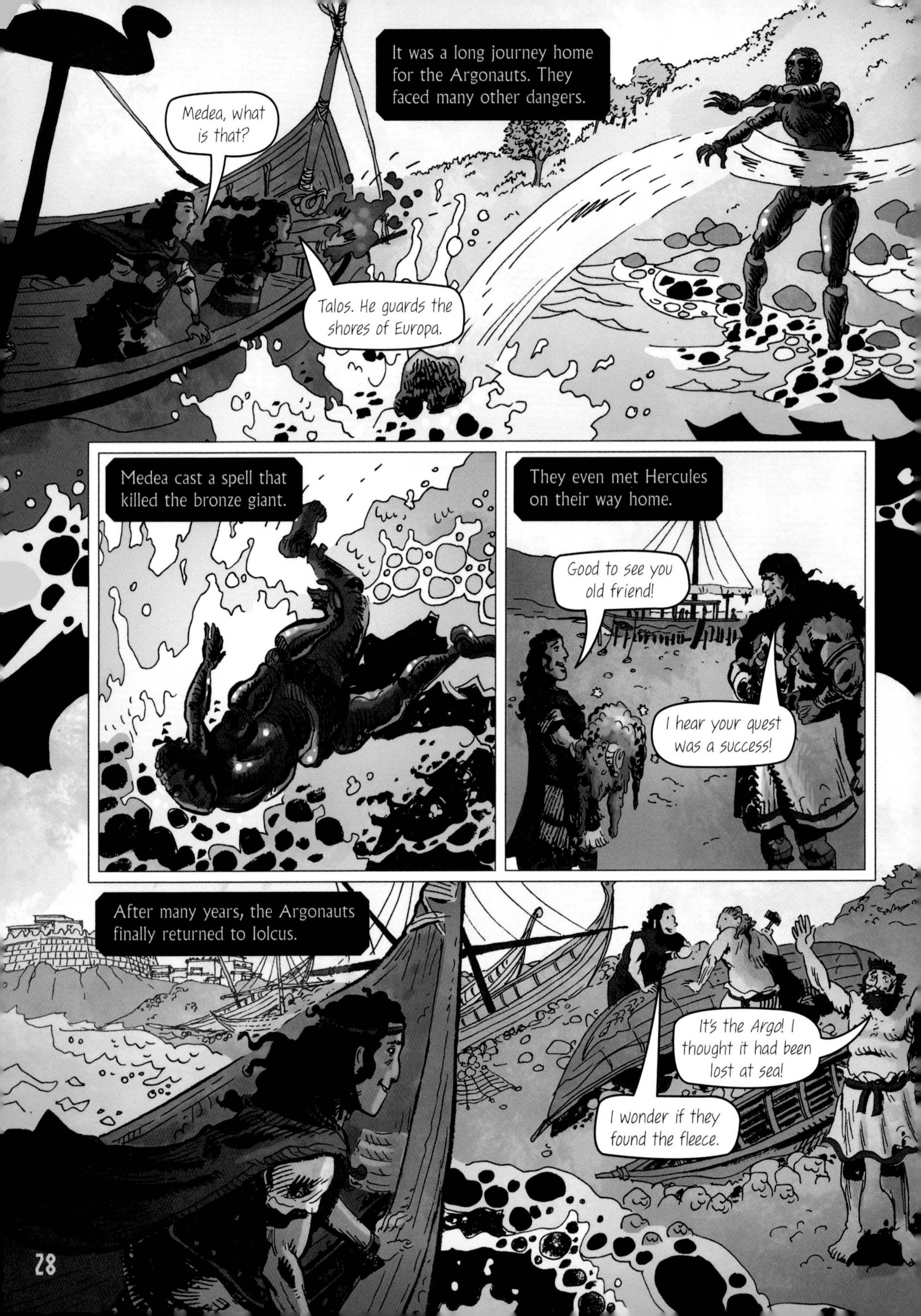
It was a long journey home for the Argonauts. They faced many other dangers.
Medea, what is that?
Talos. He guards the shores of Europa.
Medea cast a spell that killed the bronze giant.
They even met Hercules on their way home.
Good to see you old friend!
I hear your quest was a success!
After many years, the Argonauts finally returned to Iolcus.
It's the Argo! I thought it had been lost at sea!
I wonder if they found the fleece.

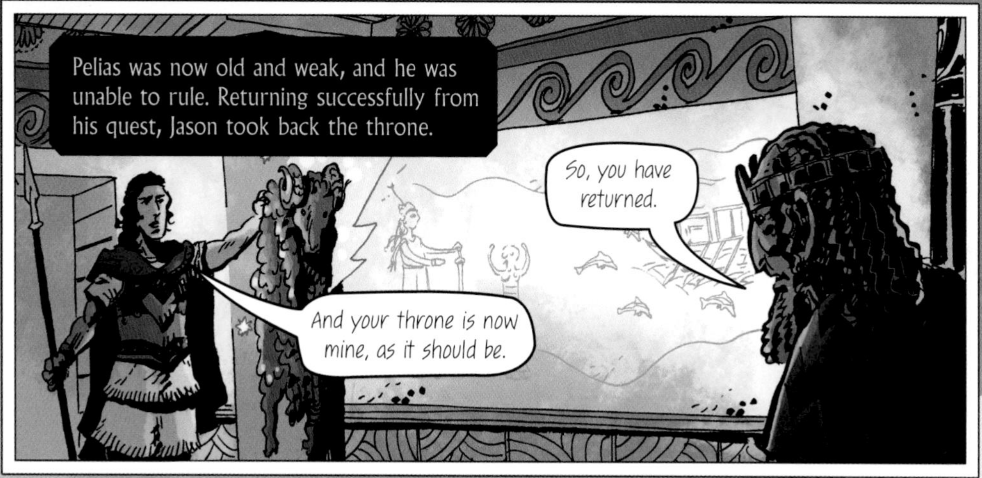
Pelias was now old and weak, and he was unable to rule. Returning successfully from his quest, Jason took back the throne.
So, you have returned.
And your throne is now mine, as it should be.

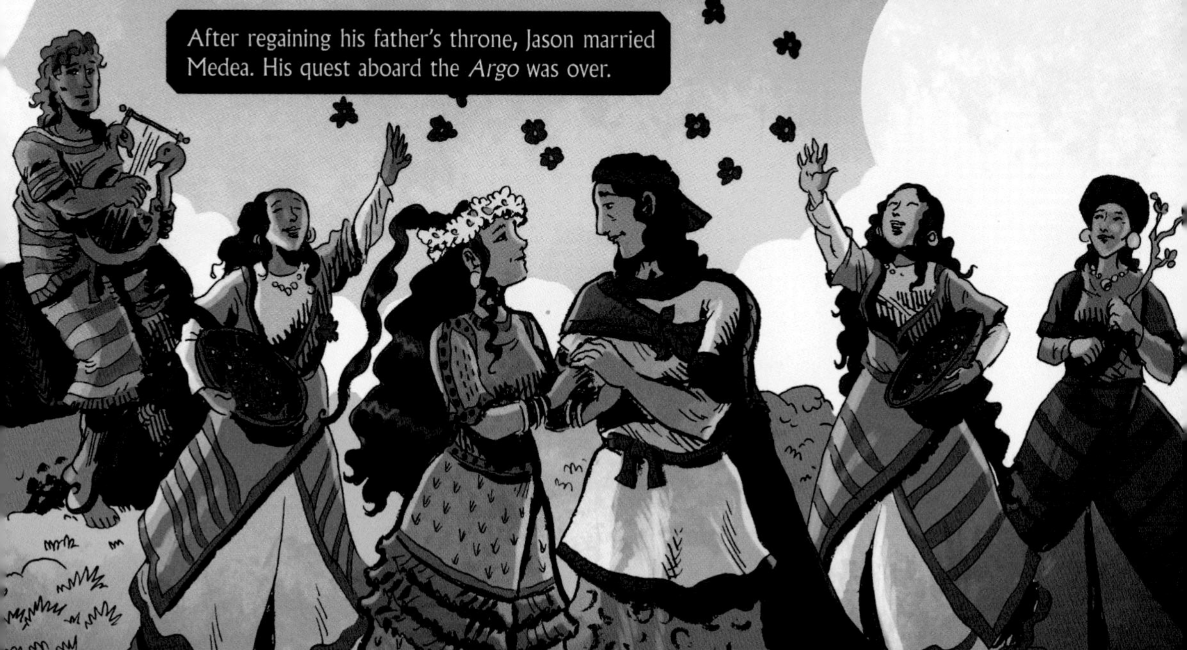
After regaining his father's throne, Jason married Medea. His quest aboard the *Argo* was over.

ANCIENT FACT

Like many heroes in ancient myths, Jason's story did not have a completely happy ending. The people of Iolcus eventually drove Jason and Medea out of the city. They were frightened by Medea's magic. After fleeing, Jason and Medea separated. Medea fled to Athens, where she met King Aegeus. Jason would return to Iolcus years later to regain his throne.

GLOSSARY

character (KAR-ik-tur)—the type of person someone is, whether that is generous or selfish, good or evil

fleece (FLEESS)—the woolly covering of a sheep

furrow (FUR-roh)—a long, narrow trench dug by a plow

oracle (OR-uh-kuhl)—in ancient myths, a person who could interpret the future

prophecy (PRAH-fuh-see)—a prediction

quest (KWEST)—a long journey to perform a task or find something

sorceress (SOR-sur-uhss)—a woman who can perform magic

sow (SOH)—to plant seeds

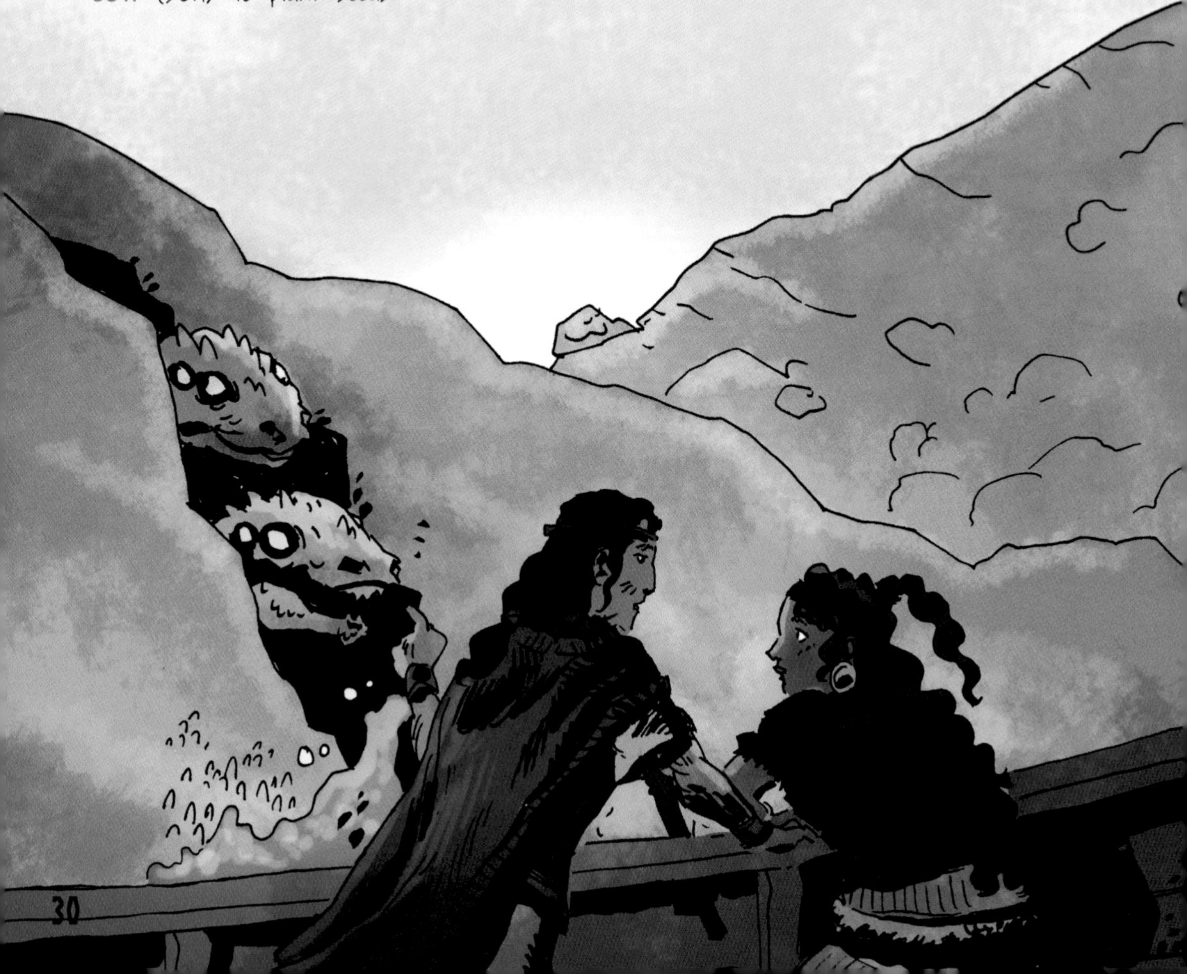

READ MORE

Baumann, Susan K. *Jason and the Golden Fleece.* Jr. Graphic Myths: Greek Heroes. New York: PowerKids Press, 2014.

Hoena, Blake. *Everything Mythology.* National Geographic Kids. Washington, D.C.: National Geographic Children's Books, 2014.

Jeffrey, Gary. *Jason and the Argonauts.* Graphic Mythical Heroes. New York: Gareth Stevens Pub., 2013.

Temple, Teri. *Hera: Queen of the Gods, Goddess of Marriage.* Mankato, Minn.: Childs World, 2013.

INTERNET SITES

FactHound offers a safe, fun way to find Internet sites related to this book. All of the sites on FactHound have been researched by our staff.

Here's all you do:

Visit *www.facthound.com*

Type in this code: 9781491420720

 **Super-cool stuff!** Check out projects, games and lots more at **www.capstonekids.com**

INDEX

TITLES IN THIS SET

A GRAPHIC RETELLING
THE 12 LABORS OF
HERCULES

A GRAPHIC RETELLING
JASON
AND THE ARGONAUTS

A GRAPHIC RETELLING
THE VOYAGE OF
ODYSSEUS

A GRAPHIC RETELLING
THE ADVENTURES OF
PERSEUS

A GRAPHIC RETELLING
THESEUS
AND THE MINOTAUR

A GRAPHIC RETELLING
THE
TROJAN WAR

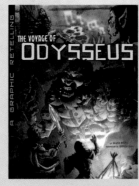